Anonymous

A Life misspent

A Series of Letters to and on the above

Anonymous

A Life misspent
A Series of Letters to and on the above

ISBN/EAN: 9783337108649

Printed in Europe, USA, Canada, Australia, Japan

Cover: Foto ©ninafisch / pixelio.de

More available books at **www.hansebooks.com**

MR W. E. GLADSTONE

A Life Misspent

A SERIES OF LETTERS TO AND ON THE ABOVE

BY

✸ ✸ ✸

ALL RIGHTS RESERVED

LONDON
SIMPKIN, MARSHALL, HAMILTON, KENT & CO. LIMITED
1893

INTRODUCTORY LETTER

To Patriots and to Radicals.

The following thirteen letters need no justification; without malice, they are written on the Right Hon. W. E. Gladstone. Their aim is to rouse the British, lest the safety and prosperity of the Empire be dreamed, dabbled, and gambled away.

The letters deal with the Politician, Statesman, Prime Minister.

Mr. W. E. Gladstone, D.C.L., as a husband and father, as a private friend and neighbour, as a landlord, even as a student and scholarly author, merits respectful consideration, and the moralist's unreserved approbation.

Mr. W. E. Gladstone as a 'financier' is perhaps worthy of some praise.

However, Mr. W. E. Gladstone as the member of Parliament, the publicist, the pamphleteer, the Party leader, the Secretary of State, the Prime Minister!

As such, he is another man. In *these* various characters he has, by his inconsistencies and vagaries, made himself almost unique. The disturbance often caused by their mere announcement seems to justify that the friends of the country not only behold them with awe, but think of their ultimate effects with vivid apprehension.

Mr. Gladstone lives in the Nineteenth century, and, indeed, he may consider himself fortunate for that. Thanks to the heroic efforts of former patriots, the fundamental principles of the Constitution of England are defined; they are fixed and well known. The consciousness of this stability and the fear of this universal knowledge somewhat restrain beforehand any would-be violators and usurpers. Moreover, on the one side, the Press, that palladium of our liberties, and *the* powerful factor in civilisation, paralyses, as it were, unconsciously and most times unknown to the beguiled or lethargic Nation, the efforts of a master-schemer in politics and supreme dabbler in diplomacy. On the other hand, science has softened the tempers of the people, so that peculiar originals, however perverse, ay, dangerous their actions may be, are treated nowadays with a certain commiserative consideration. Whether they offend against the laws, violate morals or customs, usurp or dispose of other men's property or injure the person; so long as their actions appear sufficiently eccentric, they are held to be suffering from a cerebral aberration or psychical disease. Free from any responsibility for their deeds, they not unfrequently become even idolised.

Otherwise any such extraordinary politician and fatalistically strange statesman had been dealt with in the sixteenth and seventeenth centuries. It is known that Ministers were then impeached for having sold, ceded, or diplomatically squandered away even as little as a conquered town that formed part of the Empire, though for ever so short a period. It may, therefore, be justly doubted if 'attainder,' 'impeachment,' 'pains and penalties' would have been thought by the patriots of those times sufficiently efficacious against the author of a policy which meditates the surrender of Egypt, the desertion of India, the abandonment of the Australian Colonies, the deliverance of Constantinople, the *betrayal* of Ireland. For instance :—

The patriots of those times would have argued: France impetuously demands our withdrawal from Egypt. She bases her request upon principles of International Law. Yet she herself has violated more than once such principles whenever her interests required their repudiation. As to the Egyptian territory, the French have fought battles and waged costly wars for its possession. Again, France holds Cochin China and Tonquin. Both are close to India, where she had ruled before her expulsion by the English, the present occupiers of that country. Also, France is historically proved to be the rival, thus the natural enemy of the British Nation. Her exertions for the evacuation of Egypt by the English troops is, therefore, evidence of the great importance the French people attach to the possession of the Nile Valley and Suez Canal. It indicates that *these two are the gate to the East, hence the gate to India.* From which follows that whosoever succeeds in making himself its keeper, may rule or reconquer with safety all and any of these Eastern territories. The patriots of the sixteenth and seventeenth centuries would accordingly have declared the author of such a pernicious suicidal policy, which could contemplate or actually advocate the evacuation of Egypt, thereby deserting India and abandoning the

Australian colonies, a dangerous enemy and a traitor to his country.

With respect to Constantinople those patriots would have considered:

Russia covets that city, by the occupation of which she could not fail soon to possess the remaining Turkish possessions in Europe and Asia Minor. Now, the prestige of such a conquest would make her not only the independent mistress of the Dardanelles and Black Sea, but lay Persia and Afghanistan at her mercy. This should render her influence in Asia all-powerful, extending not only over Armenia and the neighbouring countries situated close to Egypt and the Red Sea, but also over the Indian Empire. To abandon Turkey, therefore, in her resistance to Russian aggression were folly, as well as cowardly betrayal. Actually to desert her in a war with her enemy, hopeless, without help from allies, would be self-destruction. In its final results it were tantamount to a deliverance of important, vitally important Eastern dependencies of Great Britain into the occupation of Russia, another natural enemy of the English people. The patriots of the sixteenth and seventeenth centuries would accordingly have declared the author of such a pernicious policy a dangerous enemy, and a traitor to his country.

With regard to the Australian Colonies, and especially as to Ireland—but the parallel had here better be discontinued. The friends of the Nation, condemned to live in these unhappy times, can have no difficulty when remembering the patriots of the sixteenth and seventeenth centuries, in imagining what they would have thought of, and how they would have proceeded against the author of a policy of disintegration and separation. *Sapienti sat.*

However, there remain the nineteenth-century 'fin de siècle' Radicals.

It is to their reputed impartial and passionless judgment that the following letters are deferentially submitted.

In 'substance' and principles being comet-like, in nature animal; in their life-instinct materialistic—their commenting effusions are certain to be both entertaining and instructive. To behold and to hear the mob and its 'aristocratic' mouthpiece, the democratic radical Liberals, writhing and squeaking and yelling in the throes of 'argumentative' vituperations will furnish the best object-lesson to the 'evolutionist' student of zoological monstrosities. The

'Darwinian' philologist will rejoice in the prospect of finding in their language further proofs of the descent of man from the beast. And the 'sophistic' philosopher will gain valuable experience from the not unfrequent spectacle that the Radical disciples become the traducers of their Grand Old Charmer, yet whom they were eager to justify, to exalt, ay, to canonise. Already the performances given by the Right Honourable and his Honourable though somewhat rebellious satellite, Labouchere, however little developed as yet, are most curious, and certainly full of hopeful promise. . . ! For, if such things happen amongst friends, between aiders and abettors ! . . . . ?

But it is time that the epistolary portraits speak.

They are the true and truthful Positive of Mr. Gladstone, the politician, the statesman, the diplomat. If the features they exhibit are found to be harsh, if the criticisms thereon are bitter, if the impressions which these will leave with the readers are disquieting—the better for Great Britain; it is Mr. Gladstone who is both cause and effect.

Well might it be pleaded that his advanced age should call forth the utmost kindness and respectful consideration. And, indeed, where is he to be found who would refuse him, as a *private man*, almost Spartan deference?

But, old as he is, he has scornfully deserted the sanctuary of *private life*; he has gone forth to lead the destiny of *the Nation*. By an abnormal proposal he endangers the *very* existence of *the Empire*. He thus challenges *criticism*, aye, he boldly stirs *up a torrent of passions and* defiantly *provokes acrimosity—deadly* hatred. Should such *criticism be* withheld, such opposition be restrained, and Great Britain be wrecked, because he, the wrecker, is of an advanced age?

'*De mortuis nil nisi bonum*' *is a precept of* Christian *charity*. But *Mr. Gladstone*, though it *is* true *by only a brief* span *of time* separated from Eternity; he is still alive and under his tread the Empire *shakes to its very foundations*.

* * *

LONDON, *March* 1893.

LETTERS

TO THE

RIGHT HON. W. E. GLADSTONE, M.P.

> Come, come, and sit you down; you shall not budge,
> You go not, till I set you up a glass
> Where you may see the inmost part of you

CONTENTS

	PAGE
FIRST LETTER:—	
Mighty Changes within the Span of One Life	1
SECOND LETTER:—	
The Consistency of a Conscience	9
THIRD LETTER:—	
The Right Honourable and his Enemies	19
FOURTH LETTER:—	
The Right Honourable and the British Constitution	35
FIFTH LETTER:—	
The Right Honourable and the House of Lords	55
SIXTH LETTER:—	
The Right Honourable and the House of Commons and Electorate	79
SEVENTH LETTER:—	
The Right Honourable—the Diplomat and the Patriot or Foreign Policy	91

CONTENTS

	PAGE
EIGHTH LETTER:—	
THE RIGHT HONOURABLE AND SOCIAL PROBLEMS .	109
NINTH LETTER:—	
IRELAND: HER HISTORY UNDER THE PLANTAGENETS, TUDORS AND STUARTS WITH A VIEW TO HOME RULE	123
TENTH LETTER:—	
IRELAND UNDER THE GEORGES, UNDER WILLIAM, AND IN THE VICTORIAN ERA WITH A VIEW TO HOME RULE	147
ELEVENTH LETTER:—	
THE IRISH GLADSTONIAN ERA AND THE HOME RULE BILL OF 1886	185
TWELFTH LETTER:—	
THE IRISH GLADSTONIAN ERA AND THE HOME RULE BILL OF 1893	243
THIRTEENTH LETTER:—	
THE HOME RULE BILL'S EPITOME — THE RIGHT HONOURABLE'S EPITAPH?	261
INDEX	275
ADVERTISEMENT	285

FIRST LETTER

MIGHTY CHANGES WITHIN THE SPAN OF ONE LIFE

To the Right Hon. W. E. Gladstone, M.P.

Sir,—You have arrived at an age when man generally turns his mind from worldly concerns, and lives henceforth unto himself, that he may have peace hereafter. How truly it is said, therefore, that the life of man is like the passage of the sun, most beautiful when rising and when setting. But there are times when he vanishes in a welkin pregnant with thunder and fire, so that before the fretful eyes of mankind the planet of joy and light appears and disappears—a comet and a herald of commotion and dissolution.

Sir, to ask you to inquire within yourself in which of these two shapes your descent will be viewed by the nations would be adding insult, perhaps, to injustice. To assume that whilst you employ your last strength in schemes and plots which must ruin your country you are all the time firmly believing your acts to be wise and useful were to tax you with something worse than a peculiarly weak intellect. To think that you are thus strangely conducting yourself with consciousness of your exploits and with forethought would be accusing you of treason.

However, though this problem may be properly left to that Judge who alone can discern unerringly the heart and mind of man, the Nation and every citizen affected by your doings have a title to criticise their nature; and, if injured by them, the people and the individual possess not only the right to condemn their origin and purport, but further, to resist their effects. Also, so far from making it difficult your extraordinary career has rendered criticism very easy.

Commencing your political escapades under the protection of Toryism, you close it under the red flag of disintegration.

In that you fell from one extreme to the other your conduct might yet be excusable: turncoats amongst politicians are not too uncommon a species. It is comprehensible that a 'Wentworth' should develop into an 'Earl of Strafford,' and that the Mirabeau of the 'Salle de Jeu de Paume' should so far be whirled round as to finish by worshipping at Versailles: flies and moths are attracted by glitter and light.

But how must posterity start at the mentioning of a man, who, when young and out of place, posed as the *non plus ultra* champion of the worst of despotisms—the ecclesiastical, political absolutism; who afterwards, when with the help of his less cunning protectors he had climbed the ladder to power half way, assumes the opportune *rôle* of a preacher and defender of the then 'current' liberty; who, finally, when the too emotional heart and but half-grown understanding of the people were sufficiently confused and corrupted, throws off this cast for that character almost indescribable—the liberal-radical advocate of Democratic tyranny or license! Indeed, posterity will start at the sound of such a man's name; the present generation must behold him with consternation, and the peoples abroad speak of his deeds with scorn and apprehension.

And yet even therein one might pardon your conduct; its very perverseness pleads in your favour; it is psychologically unaccountable.

Though—you are not charged, because you

could not conform with the ordinary course of nature in that 'enthusiasm for some sort of liberty is generally found in youth, and love for law and order in old age.' Also, it were presumption, nay, usurpation of a right, and violation of two sacred principles: the *actor sequitur rei forum* and *extra territorium jus dicendi impune non paretur*—; if other than your fellow-members should impeach you for actions which bear a fatal resemblance to conspiracy, incitement to riot and high treason. And the representatives of the English Nation cannot already be unnerved to such an extent that they should be afraid to remember and, if need be, to apply, how their ancestors have dealt with all those who plotted the dismemberment of the Empire and the corruption of the people. Indeed, you read history, although, true to your character even in this, you read it most peculiarly; such instances of bitter resentment against notorious agitators, disintegrators and traitors, on the part of a just, generous, free and patriotic people, may thus, notwithstanding your predilection for perversion, not be unknown to you.

But when the rule of courtesy and decency towards, and the law of respect for others than your unhappy country are alarmingly violated by you; when, not content to cast the brand of disorder and revolt in the homesteads of hitherto peaceable and contented citizens, you raise the banner of sedition among misguided tribes of foreign nations; when, not satisfied with having set an awful example by your alliance with the Healyites of countenancing mutilation, arson, revolt and murder *at home*, you dare to preach, or, at least, to patronise, such pernicious doctrines *abroad*, and boastfully to receive the acclamations of Czechs and other would-be rebels: then, sir, when you appear to be the recognised chief of all the outlawed and the lawless of Europe, then is the time, when against an international evil, international remedies should and must be used with all despatch and energy.

Beware! Foreign governments will know how to safeguard the welfare and how to protect the property and integrity of their citizens; the measures of these governments against your country will fall back with double force on your past and future.

The English are generous. Moved by your age and their sanguine temperament easily beguiled by promises, they have, in an abuse of their generosity, returned you to power. Take care lest they be shaken too roughly out of their noxious dream by a worse reality; by your actions, which your enemies would impeach as unlawful, you might be held to have placed yourself outside the *constitutional* pale of the law.

SECOND LETTER

THE CONSISTENCY OF A CONSCIENCE

To the Right Hon. W. E. Gladstone, M.P.

SIR,—But a few more days, and you will have reached the zenith of your ambitions: you will be at the head of the affairs of Great Britain. That explains the enthusiasm and activity suddenly displayed by her most bitter enemies; they rely on the contradiction of your nature.

However, you are not so much impeached here for your conduct towards the Maynooth Bill, the Australian Colonies Bill and my Lord John Russell's Ecclesiastical Titles Bill.

Though inconsistent in your notions, utterances and actions, you were at that time a Peelite, and what is even more, a Puseyite. Thus, as it were, privileged continually to change and betray what with other men would be 'principles;' moreover, an absolutist in matters religious, you could with some decorum on the one side support the claims and assumptions of Church of England Episcopacy upon the colonies; on the other, defend the Papal usurpation of English territories.

Sir, it is your subsequent conduct which might justify the joy of Great Britain's enemies over your ascendency; which certainly has marked you one of the greatest calamities that may befall a nation.

Once attached to Doellinger, the absolute and infallible Pope's archfoe, and with him great in invoking the wrath of the Lord against Popery and the Vatican Council, you are now prepared even to wade through Civil War, if only you succeed in delivering a brave, honest and industrious people of your faith and race into the claws of Jesuitism and 'Walshite' inquisition.

Yet your conduct even in this might be found somewhat excusable; there is a fatal consistency of evil.

You did violence to yourself and denied your character. Destined for commotion, war and disintegration, you were obstinately bent upon pursuing a policy of 'pacification' and 'indemnification.' The curse fell on your perverse actions; outraged Nature had her revenge. You, the foremost champion of Communism and

Democracy, were to match in one common misdeed the most arbitrary of princes. In 1871 you perpetrated an act that your enemies call sacrilege, and which is equalled only by the sequestration of Henry VIII.

What did it matter that you were the bold author of 'The State in its Relation to the Church,' of that hyperorthodox and absolutistic treatise in which you called heaven's vengeance upon all those who dared but utter a syllable against the Established Church of your country —the Twin Sister of which, notwithstanding, a few years afterwards none other than you should doom to die? What could it matter that you were the man who for the sake of that book actually forsook his post in the Cabinet and deserted the Board of Trade at a moment most critical, under circumstances which, but for the favour of Providence, might have become most disastrous to the Nation? Of what consequence could it be to you that you betrayed in the face of the world your patron and friend and almost involved the downfall of your leader and Party, all this for the reputation of theories, for the sake of dogmas, yet which you *denounced by your private vote*, as it were, on the morn of their proclamation?

Sir, you were 'the purist with respect to what touches the consistency of Statesmen.' You committed that deed because your conscience and your notion of consistency revolted against a just grant to Maynooth of a few thousand pounds for the education of Irish priests. In the same manner it happened that twenty-five years later you were goaded by this consistent conscience to deprive the faithful sister of your Church of hundreds of thousands for the support of those very priestly agitators.

Indeed, it was consistent! That the Nation stood bewildered, that the English could not understand this positively morbid, almost fantastic over-scrupulosity is comprehensible. That Sir R. Peel employed you again in the following year is explainable. This statesman had already arrived at such perfection in betraying his friends, constituents and clients, that he could not fail to appreciate the rapid development of a similar tendency in a nature, in a character so wonderfully congenial to his as he found yours. And did you not throw up office in a like manner a few years later from a most morbid perverseness of consistency and conscience? Did you not abandon the Chancellorship of the Exchequer from a strange antagonism against Mr. Roebuck's motion for an inquiry into the state of the British Army before Sebastopol, though that investigation was demanded in the interests of charity, humanity, honour and patriotism ? Your friends, my Lords John Russell and Palmerston, had every reason to remember your fits of puristic consistency of those times. (See pages 102, 103.)

Sir, your conduct recalls Horace's 'Furorne cæcus, an rapit vis acrior, an culpa?' To you seems addressed 'Sic est, acerba fata te agunt.' Thus, the world may believe that, though a willing, yet you were a mere tool in the schemes of your country's evil destiny, and you may be pitied. Moreover, Rome has always claimed the power to absolve people for the celestial Eldorado, and the burden of your past must disquiet your expectations of a future; great men are known to be superstitious. Above all, for once you have shown a certain tact; your friend is dead; so is Pius IX., and Rome is in the ascendant.

The murder of the hero of Khartum, however, justifies England's enemies no longer to doubt your code of morals, but boldly to hope and brazenly to demand from you even the final betrayal of your Nation.

The bones of that great patriot, brave man, and one of the bravest soldiers are scarcely paled by Egypt's glowing sun, and the widows and orphans consoled for the loss of their husbands and fathers, slain in her 'necessary' conquest and afterwards 'vital' defence; and you can contemplate the surrender of this your country's only gate to India!

That you have forgotten the memorable words of the Czar Nicholas, the then ruler of your country's bitter enemies is pardonable. You have reason to shun the remembrance of those times. But the debates on Sir Michael Hicks-Beach's motion relative to the hero General Gordon and the acclamations of the Australian Colonies ought, if not to touch your conscience, at least to tingle still in your ears.

Sirrah! Coquetry in youth, though blamable, is yet tolerable. Coquetry in old age, when in a woman is ludicrous; if in a man, it is contemptible and detestable. Yet when an octogenarian politician appears to coquet away one of the foremost possessions of the Nation, because the country of the Zolas, the Proudhons, the Renans supports by its morals and political excesses the propagation of *his* political creed, which to all and every uninitiated person justly seems to be 'corruptive,' 'treasonable,' 'destructive'—he must be held to be either an enemy of his country or a dangerous fanatic. But you shall hear yet more of Egypt.

There can be no doubt you learnt Sophocles' ' πολλὰ τὰ δεινὰ κοὐδὲν ἀνθρώπου δεινότερον πέλει ' too well, and on beholding your deeds your foes might think of Milton's description—'with thoughts inflamed of highest design; he put on swift wings, and towards the gates of hell explored his solitary flight.' In fact, on the eve of your days your enemies maintain, you could almost in the words of Mirabeau, say to your unhappy Nation: 'My life, full of depredations and injustice, has opened an abyss into which the kingdom is doomed to fall, and where it must perish. But, before I depart, let us yet try to fill it. Here is a list of proprietors, of middle-class citizens and gentry; select the wealthiest, the best educated, the most talented, it is just that the classes shall die for the masses. Then, triumph Democracy, i.e. Tyranny or Anarchy!—Communism, i.e. Licentiousness!'

Sir, this peroration, not at all inconsistent with the political record of utterances and deeds of the human author of the 'Letters from Naples,' and fully in harmony with the sentiments of the Russian servile 'patron' of the Bulgarian horrors, might be held to be consistent with the organiser, and especially with the *purveyor* of the Crimean and Egyptian campaigns on the one side—and the coercive legislator; then, apostate and apologist of Fenianism on the other. Aye, the world expected yet to see Mr. Gladstone and Michael Davitt, a second 'modernised' edition of Absalom and Ahithophel, fight shoulder to shoulder for their ideals—disintegration of the Empire and Irish-English Republics.

But ' μεγίστη δ' ἔλπις ἐν τοῖς πολέμοις ἐστὶ τὸ δίκαιον.'

There are ethics for the course of man as for that of nations. A career, begotten by treacherous ambition and pursued with the help of iniquity and injustice, conceives at its very outset the curse of ruin and self-destruction. Of such a man might be said, 'When gloom has swallowed up the Universe, then he will stand confronted with Immensity, a lonely ghost amid a desert, where nought else but the ghastly ruins of his country shall be his wake and sleep companions.'

THIRD LETTER

THE RIGHT HONOURABLE AND HIS ENEMIES

To the Right Hon. W. E. Gladstone, M.P.

Sir,—Your enemies say that you hunger after infallible dictatorship. They charge you with defection. They proclaim you as a being possessed by the demon of destruction. Looking upon your career, they call you the personified contradiction and perverseness. Above all, as you know, they accuse you of treason.

Though your enemies base their charges not so much upon your betrayal of whole provinces which form parts, important parts of the Empire; yet of proofs they could not be wanting. Amongst many, they need only point to your treachery towards the loyal South African colonists.

Neither do they impeach you on account of the vituperations which you generally cast on your 'cats-paws,' as, for instance, at 'a certain Mr. Jesse Collings.' Remembering that it is the Right Honourable W. E. Gladstone, your enemies expect that after having effectively and sometimes not very honestly used your tools, you positively deny all connection with them. Indeed, in you it is natural that whenever *their*, to say the least, unscrupulous actions, although committed for your sake and upon your insinuation, or rather instigation, are likely to bring in jeopardy your *own* reputation of self-just consciousness and hyper-conscientious righteousness :—you should at once deliver up your tools to the wrath of your reviled and injured rivals.

Again, there stand counts against you, charging you directly with moral assassinations. But here, too, your enemies forbear to indict you, notwithstanding that those so-called moral assassinations have not unfrequently entailed the premature physical death of your victims. Your enemies pretend to be guided in their moderation by considerations of 'public policy.' For instance, they condemn your conduct towards Charles Stewart Parnell, the once by you much-wooed aider and abettor in your plot for the destruction of the Empire by treasonable disintegration. But they are apprehensive lest, in impeaching you for the ruin of the Irish leader, they should impeach your accomplice in treason, Dr. Walsh. It is for morality's sake that they threaten such an indictment.

They know that your undoubtedly most puristic sentiments in Church and Irish-English politics are the mere echo of that prelate's instructions. They are aware that this your anointed confederate implores the heavens for either the conversion or annihilation of your apostate country. They are convinced that in case of a conflict between England and the Vatican or any holy-Popish-Catholic state, your would-be Cardinal-associate would side against your country, even after his installation as Irish Pope by your Home Rule scheme. For these very reasons your enemies justly fear that a trial against you and your accomplice, the archiepiscopal dictator of Ireland, might call forth revelations the publication of which could not fail for ever to corrupt the still existing moral instincts of the Nation.

Moreover, your enemies hold that the premature death of the uncrowned king, as well as the 'Machiavellic' intrigues from the 'Pact of Kilmainham' to the conspiracy at 'Committee Room, No. 15,' have already become historic. They are of opinion that these events came to pass quite naturally—inevitably.

Charles Stewart Parnell appears in matters politic to have acted from somewhat reasonable and in several points, excusable motives. The uncrowned king was an Irish agitator. As such he looked upon the English as his foes. As such he struggled and plotted for what he believed to be his country's good. As such it was that he attempted the ruin of what he believed to be his country's evil—the ruin of England—of Great Britain.

But you, the Right Hon. W. E. Gladstone, are supposed to be an English 'statesman!' Thus, what motives your enemies ask, could *you* have to aid and abet that Irishman in his endeavours to establish in the Emerald Isle a new 'tyrannis'? It was scarcely possible that you, the great Statesman and prophet in the wilderness of politics, were alone unconscious of their purport. The instinct of patriotism in every other Briton revolted against these acts of the uncrowned king. It was universally felt that they aimed at the destruction of England. Still you, your enemies exclaim, you were actually plotting with Fenians and Land Leaguers at the very time when the English Nation had chosen you Great Britain's—England's—Prime Minister, to protect her property, to defend her honour, to maintain her laws, to preserve her order and peace, and thus to further her welfare and prosperity.

Your revilers, it is true, say that the implacable hatred which your actions suggest you bear your country, prove that you are Welsh, that you are Scotch, that you are Irish, that you are even French, aye, Russian, rather than English. But though—your enemies maintain that having been born in and educated, nursed and enriched by England, any other moral character than you would ethically, logically and materially belong to such a motherly country.

This patriotism it is, your enemies argue, that constituted Parnell's crime. They say his independence and power were like a poisonous two-edged dagger in your heart, diseased by constantly revelling in visions of lusty, unrestrained dictatorship. They are of opinion that it was this very patriotism and sagaciously independent spirit which ennobled the actions and motives of the uncrowned king when compared with your schemes and with what your enemies call: your unparalleled misdeeds. Hence, they maintain, sprung the hatred which you conceived against your trusty ally, Charles Stewart Parnell. Hence the eagerness with which you seized the opportunity to ruin him, when for once a docile imitator, the Irish leader betrayed a friend in private life. Sir, you may well believe your enemies were not surprised that your sense of righteousness and propriety should be so indignantly tickled by it. They expected that you would instantly take up your old game. They had seen you at it before, and they knew that in *defence of* morality you would not hesitate to revile and betray your accomplice. They perfectly understood that you could not do otherwise than punish this Parnell who so foolishly allowed his weakness to be uncloaked before that farrago of religion, before that self-righteous hydra of dissenting prayer-clubs, before those Methodists, Congregationalists and Tabernaclists who, next to the Irish archpriests, were then dearest to your heart.

Indeed, your enemies were not startled when in alliance with these Irish archpriests you exhorted the Tim Healyites to revolt against the uncrowned king. It is true you and the world knew that through him not a few of them had been raised to lucrative and glittering agitatorships from a state, morally, intellectually, and, perhaps, in most cases, materially *indigent*. But the world had also learnt the O'Shea failing of your brother in conspiracy and helpmate in contriving the ruin of your country. For you, therefore, to preach to them there and then on such ethics as gratitude, would have been not only absurd but most unnatural. Sir, you understood your duties towards your country far better. You knew that on you and on you alone it became incumbent to avenge outraged purism. Inspired by morality you at once comprehended that none but *you* could despatch with a final sanctimonious stab your already wounded, at one time by you obsequiously served and much trusted aider and abettor. The fact was, to repeat it, Parnell's usefulness had ceased. His patriotism shamed you. His merits and abilities overshadowed yours. His consistency, and from an Irishman's standpoint, comprehensible and justifiable fixed purpose when compared with your perverseness and opportuneness, were hateful to you. His ambition threatened your rapacity. There was danger that his exposure might involve yours. Above all, he was your accomplice in your political misdeeds. And you know that, in spite of their cant, criminals are said to shun, even deadly to hate their associates in crime after its commission. It devolved upon you, therefore, to act. And your enemies admit that you did act. They took it as a matter of course when you issued to these Tim Healy-ites, '*whose footsteps had hitherto been dogged by crime,*' the worldly famous, ethically infamous mandate: undo him, betray him, nay, tear him *bodily* to pieces, if only morality be saved for the country. Ah, sir, morality! Your enemies say you certainly enriched by your 'apostolic' epistle to Justin McCarthy the literature on ethics in politics and on morals among prayer-clubs and priest-leagues.

Sir, the accusation which is hurled at you by your enemies is far more galling. It is of a most ignominious nature. They charge you not only with Popery and Jesuitism, but also with perfidious, ungrateful cowardice.

Yet with respect to the first count! Is it that your enemies forget your illustrious career as the melodramatic Scripture reader of the Church of England? Is it that they look upon your partisans' Sunday pilgrimages to the Hawarden Chapel as being naught else than a big farce, adapted from the Church of Rome shows by some wire-pullers for the statesman-actor? Or is it that they wrongfully appreciate your exploits as the Church of England 'master-jongleur?' Is it that they falsely construe the pamphlets, tracts, and bulls with which you, in your capacity of the Church of England controversial dogma doctor, afflict the world?

It is true, to charge you with Popery and Jesuitism seems at first sight anomalous. Your enemies admit that the accusation *appears* to be unnatural—the proof thereof almost impossible. But they maintain, *only so at first sight.* They do not deny that you are the author of 'The Church of England, is it worth Preserving?' of 'The Vatican Decrees in their Bearing on Civil Allegiance,' of 'Vaticanism.' Yet they point out that you are also the author of the 'Irish Disestablishment Bill' and the 'Irish University Bill.' Further, they comment on the strange coincidence that your bosom friends were Hope, Newman and Manning, all three Roman converts, or, from a Protestant's view, Apostates, Papists, and certainly the deadliest enemies of the Church of England. Again, your adversaries acknowledge that you wrote 'What is Ritualism?'; but they interpret its meaning by your conduct towards the 'Public Worship Regulation Bill,' as well as towards the 'Endowed Schools Act Amendment Bill.' Therefore, you cannot wonder that they call you the ecclesiastical broker. However, it is on account of your duplicity **whenever there are** motions in the **House of** Commons for the Disestablishment **of the** Church of Scotland, or of **the** so-called Church of Wales, or of the **Church of** England, and because of your contradictory, though 'cunning' platform utterances thereon, that your enemies denounce you the 'opportunist arch-Jesuit.' **And** they argue that in criminal matters for instance, any evil-doer with such a record, although charged on suspicion only, would unhesitatingly be convicted.

As to the second count, that of cowardice, your enemies do not forget how boldly you have always defended the pretensions, insults and injuries which the mob and the home and foreign foes of **Great** Britain inflict on the unhappy Nation, on your betrayed country. They admit that you brazen anything, even when out of office, so long as you can harm England. However, in all other circumstances they contend, you are the slave of the intimidating influences of a troubled conscience, except when you are goaded by some individual hatred. As proof, your enemies advance that in times of turmoil and peril you desert the **party** which has made you what you **are.** They say that you act thus from cowardice. But they go farther. They search for a second reason why at such critical moments you betray those who—when one considers your career—entrusted and entrust with a *most touching simplicity* their 'ideals' or 'idols,' their welfare or success, their honour or reputation, their glory or conceit, even their very existence and future into your honest, firm, consistent and circumspect care. Sir, your enemies assert that you retire at those crises to your Hawarden Tusculum in order better to gloat over the havoc wrought by your ambitious misdeeds among your brethren, disciples, retainers and followers. They call your pretext that you 'seclude' yourself in your retreat for *the purpose of studying* 'Homer or ecclesiastical legerdemain' a mere imposture. In support of their allegations they point to the history of your memorable abdication of the leadership of the great 'conglomerate' Liberal party in 1875, in favour of your friend, my Lord Hartington. But in this your enemies apparently forget that an individual diseased and devoured by the lust of and for power, inasmuch as it is abnormal, must be guided by a code of abnormal morals, peculiar to his peculiar instincts. They forget that to be the leader of a party which unfortunate events have driven into a hopeless opposition, requires a character sincere, firm and patriotic. They naïvely think that an honest and true statesman would exult in the prospect of, and render thanks to the Deity for having been chosen to lead his partisans safely through the adversities to victory and triumph. They charge you with an insatiable greed for power, yet seemingly do not take into account that the leadership of a party placed in an apparently hopeless opposition is barren in conceit, adulation, patronages, sinecures, benefices, and what might be called 'ministerialties.' Above all, they forget your letter to my Lord Granville, dated January 14, 1875, and for once unmistakably explanatory of your abdication; the letter in which you wrote: 'The time has, I think, arrived, when I ought to return to the subject of the letter which I addressed to you on March 12. Before determining whether I should offer to assume a charge (i.e. the leadership) which might extend over a length of time, I have reviewed, with all the care in my power, a number of considerations, both public and private. . . . *The result has been that I see no public advantage in my continuing to act as the leader of the Liberal party; and that, at the age of sixty-five, and after forty-two years of a laborious public life, I think myself entitled to retire on the "present" opportunity. This retirement is dictated to me by my "present" personal views as to the best method of spending the closing years of my life.'* . . .

It is :—they have since seen you twice reappear on the field of action, in the midst of the turmoil of factions, where there is certainly not preached the Evangel of God and Eternity but the gospel of the world; and they have lost their faith in the sincerity of your decisions. Indeed, when contemplating what your personal views 'as to the best method of spending the closing years of your life' have been from then until your Second Home Rule Scheme, they justly hold that not only their former count against you is right, but that for your epitaph might be used Ben Jonson's 'Fall of Catiline:'

> Which Catiline seeing, and that now his troops
> Covered the earth they 'ad fought on with their trunks,
> *Ambitious of great fame, to crown his ill
> Collected all his fury*, and ran in
> (Armed with a glory high as his despair)
> Into our battle, like a Libyan lion
> Upon his hunters, scornful of our weapons,
> Careless of wounds, plucking down lives about him,
> Till he had circled on himself with death :
> Then fell he too, t'embrace it where it lay,
> And as in that rebellion 'gainst the gods,

> Minerva holding forth Medusa's head,
> One of the giant brethren felt himself
> Grow marble at the killing sight ; and now,
> Almost made stone, began to inquire what flint,
> What rock, it was that crept through all his limbs ;
> And, ere he could think more, was that he fear'd
> So Catiline, *at the sight of Rome* in us,
> Became his tomb ; yet did his look retain
> Some of his fierceness, and his hands still moved,
> *As if he labour'd yet to grasp the state*
> *With those rebellious parts.*
>   Cato: A brave bad death !
> Had this been honest now, and *for his country,*
> *As 'twas against it, who had e'er fall'n greater ?*

Sir, would it be inappropriate ?

Ah, look to it ! There is one more indictment ! Your enemies think it explains all. They hold that *destruction* proves to be the mission, the *raison d'être* of your existence. They allude to the weird spectacle of the 'Statesman-woodcutter,' to which, whenever out of office, you so largely treat the Nation. And they ask : Is it : that whilst you thus practise destruction on trees and shrubs, your imagination, easily stretching, marks—in anticipation of the day when you will be returned to power—the branches which you will then cut off your Country's glorious and invaluable Constitution ?

FOURTH LETTER

THE RIGHT HONOURABLE AND THE BRITISH CONSTITUTION

To the Right Hon. W. E. Gladstone, M.P.

Sir,—The British Constitution!?

Unique as it is, it is justly considered by the patriot as synonymous with the safety, prosperity and grandeur of Great Britain.

'And yet it is no document, nor is it a statute or a code. It is neither tangible nor visible. No stones nor casements enclose it, no bayonets protect it, no circuits of entrenched posts confine it.' Like the country for which it was destined, it is free, without boundaries that might mar its majesty. Unsullied by the pedantry, egotism, prejudice, ambition, bigotry and passion of man, it is limited only by restrictions which were inspired by divine precepts and suggested by physical law.

But it is sanctioned by a thousand years. Created, wrought, framed, shaped by nature and circumstances, it has been transmitted from generation to generation as *the* blessing. Its teachings are the universal conceptions of the English Nation. Its principles are the symbol, the shibboleth, the Evangel for true English conduct—for British feelings, thoughts and actions. It is the regulator of the very life of your Nation. And this greatest of inheritances—left, transmitted, treasured up for so many ages from father to son—*it has grown to the hearts of the people whence it had sprung*; it is one with the people. Sir, to maim it! Sir, to cut it asunder *is to sap the very existence of the Empire.*

What inducements, what powerful reasons, what sacred obligations for every Briton, the highest and the lowest, the noblest and the meanest to hold it in esteem, to regard it with reverence, to love it with veneration! How deeply he must have fallen who madly attempts to conspire against it! Can he be English? Is he a man?!

But no—*you* do not attack the British Constitution. You know that your Nation, notwithstanding their party clamours against it, instinctively feel that its ruin means the ruin of the country. Bold as you are, the prospect of such a war as an honest attack would provoke appals you. So you employ a more ignoble method—you *undermine its pillars.*

There are three of these columns by which the British Empire is upheld—the Crown, or Prerogative and Executive; the House of Lords, or Veto and Legislative; the House of Commons, or the Legislative. You are acquainted with them; they bear your marks.

Yet, behold! Lest the Crown overshadow the Commons, it is checked by the Lords; lest it be crushed by the Commons, it is supported by the Lords. And in the same measure as the Upper House forms the connecting link between the Executive and Legislative, i.e. the Sovereign and the People, *the Cabinet is the common factor between Prerogative, Control and Liberty*, so that none stands solitary.

Here, then, is the ideal state of Aristotle. Here is the best government of which Polybius tells us—the constitution that consists of the three forms, *regno, optimatium, et populi imperio*: in English, Sovereign, Lords and Commoners. The mixed government of Cicero is realised in the British: Crown, Nobles and Commoners participate in the administration and development of Great Britain's Constitution. In theory they are deputed by, and symbolic of parties; in practice, they represent the whole Nation. United, they frame the laws and regulations, which, jointly and severally, they willingly bear and gladly obey.

No deadlock is to be apprehended as may happen in Switzerland, or especially in the North American Republic.

The Senate of the United States is composed of representatives of the several States; it is plutocratic-autocratic. It is its own administrator, controller and judge. The Congress consists of deputies, nominally elected by the people, actually by cliques and factions; it is impetuous, and may become licentious, being its own master.

Neither are there the dangers to which the French constitution is exposed.

The Senate of France is the assembly of sycophants of the President, of creatures of the Ministers, of promoted dependents and agents from the factions of the Chamber; of retired 'littérateurs' and professional 'politiqueurs.' Their tenure of office is nine years, renewable, however, by thirds every three years; they hold it at the pleasure of their protectors, cabals or clubs. The Chamber is the meeting-place of the ambitious, of agitators and fanatics, of place-hunters, journalists and financiers. They are paid by the people, and usually become the slaves of the mob, of the passions of their coterie, of the bigotry of their sect. France is, quite naturally, in turns the hot-bed of Pluto-oligarchy, or Ochlarchy=Ochlocraty, or Despotism.

Finally, the chances that the sovereign or his chancellor coerce or otherwise abuse the Legislature, as it occurred and occurs in Germany and Austria, are very remote, if not impossible in this country.

But, sir, you know these constitutions. They recall Cicero's *ex regno dominus; ex optimatibus factio; ex populo turba et confusio.* Hence your predilection for the *civitas popularis*, because its rapid, almost immediate development to full growth leads and terminates, naturally and nearly always, into mob tyranny and lawless confusion. Hence your great aversion to the British Constitution. It is the Constitution of law and order, of equity and moderation, of true equality. Its principle is 'one common law and one justice for all and everyone,' notwithstanding that there have happened and will happen in some particular instances exceptions of irregularity, inasmuch as man manipulates that great principle of equity—of moderation.

Here, passions and ambitions for supreme

power, exercised by an individual over the Nation must devour *themselves*; there is no vantage ground for excessive egotism, brutal licentiousness, cruel despotism. Here, the virtues of each of the three 'Estates,' the Crown, the Lords, the Commoners are called forth and brought into beneficial action. The vices of each are restrained, balanced, modified, or changed and turned to advantage by the continual jealousy and the fear of a coalition between two of the three elements for the destruction of the third. Here, even the mere thought of such a coalition being dreaded and treated as high treason, that pernicious union is impossible; the character of the people, the nature of the conditions, and the condition of the surroundings, the history of past events prevent it. The 'Estates' know that of the two surviving parties, one, in its turn, would become annihilated in an inevitable duel for the final hegemony.

Do you want proofs? No, you have read the story of France, that tale so full of convulsions, excesses, outrages and murders. Aye, your enemies, judging from your insinuations and from appearances, accuse you of nursing, as the very aim of your life, the awful desire of repeating in England within one generation that endless history. They charge you with harbouring the evil design of reproducing in this country those epochs from Louis XI. till Louis XIV., from the author of 'L'état c'est moi' to the Revolution, from the Reign of Terror until the tyranny of Napoleon. They tax you with having the wicked intention of imitating that time of the 'Sacre,' the Polignacs, the Guizots, the Lamartines, and the Louis Blancs, a time extending but a little over twenty-five years, and yet so full of deceptions, commotions and outrages. They insinuate that you do your utmost to re-enact in this country a period such as that from Louis Buonaparte till the 'Pétroleuse,' from MacMahon until Boulanger, from Boulanger to the Panama Scandals.

Yet, you may say England herself can bear testimony to Tacitus's 'cunctas nationes et urbes populus aut primores aut singuli regunt, delecta ex his et constituta reipublicæ forma laudari facilius quam evenire, vel si evenit haud diuturna esse potest.' In defence of your struggles for the triumph of democracy, i.e. turba et confusio, you may advance that, though the enemy of *honour*, the incentive to noble actions in monarchies, you are the champion of '*virtue*,' the all-moving power in republics. You may quote Montesquieu's 'la force des lois dans un gouvernement monarchique; le bras du prince toujours levé dans un gouvernement despotique, règlent et contiennent tout; mais dans un état populaire il faut un ressort de plus, qui est la vertu.' In support thereof, you may point to the Romans in the time of the elder Brutus, to the Dutch in the age of the Nassaus, to the Americans during the life of Washington.

But was Rome, at the time when Brutus delivered her from the tyranny of Tarquin, or for a century afterwards, a Democracy? Or has she ever been a 'civitas popularis'? Hear 'Polybius.' He foretells that her ruin would arise from the popular tumults. Introducing apparently the 'dominatio plebis' (the tyrannic anarchy of mob-rule) they created instantly, as it were within and conjointly with the creation of that mob-rule, the arbitrary government, if government it could be called, of a single person. Indeed, the moment the 'plebes' were predominant the freedom of Rome sank, buried in civil wars. The *virtuous*—the powerful city was the city ruled over by the aristocracy.

Or were the Dutch democratic? The burghers shared in the government, it is true.

Yet, like the members of the City of London Corporation, they had ultra 'aristocratic'—plutocratic tendencies. In fact, the Council of that nation was managed by an oligarchy. There were patricians, and there were nobles, such as the Counts of Horn and Egmont, Prince William the Silent and Maurice of Orange. Whereas, John de Witt, the great republican and democrat, the patriot and champion of his country's liberties against the aggressions of the Nassaus at a later period, was assassinated by the mob— the democracy.

Still with respect to America your argument seems to hold good.

The country, whence the declaration of the rights of man enlightened the world, and in the end set France aflame, was at the time of its rise against 'unjust' taxation animated by the true democratic spirit. It was moved by that *spirit which is so liberal when sitting in judgment on, or actually dividing and distributing other people's property;* so orthodoxly conservative when called upon to contribute its share to a fund, or to assist in an undertaking not immediately benefiting it. Such a clique, inspired by such principles, ruled this great American Rebellion, notwithstanding, or in spite of the noble Washington, and they ventured upon this secession, though ostensibly for the sake of freedom, yet actuated by egotism, goaded on by disappointed ambition, stirred by jealousy, driven by avarice. They thought it was to their material advantage to sever all connection with their mother country in order better to combat and compete with it; just as some say the Australians perceived it to be to their interest to support Great Britain in her struggle for the possession of the Suez Canal. But materialism and selfishness, the mainsprings of that American event, and always to be found in tyrants or would-be autocrats, your enemies argue, are synonymous with your 'democratic' virtue; and inasmuch as they accuse you of disparaging *honour*, they maintain that you look upon this American rebellion with loving approbation, believing yourself in interestedness as *the* powerful incentive to daring actions.

However, as to England, the England of the Tudors and Stuarts, and her glorious Constitution! Do they not prove the dictum of Tacitus?

Ah, sir, you are right in one sense; attempts at encroachments have been made. Yet look into the annals of your country. Their failures are recorded there as having always been disastrous to those who ventured upon them. Though you are not wrong.

The English Constitution was not without its 'Sturm- und Drang-Periode.'

It had to pass through vicissitudes, as everything that becomes mixed up with man has to undergo the trials and will be affected by the changes to which human nature is liable and continually subjected. However, the Witenagemote and the Witans, the Parliament and the County Councils, the Hundred Courts, the Quarter Sessions, the Town Moots, the Municipalities—are they in principle, or even structurally essentially different? 'In the days of the Saxon kings, the Lord-Lieutenants, the Sheriffs, the Justices of the Peace were not elected magistrates to do the work of their constituents but the king's servants, named by him to do the king's work, i.e. public work.' Have the character of their appointments and the nature of their functions changed during these many centuries? They are in principle almost the same now as they were then, and the Nation has thriven, lived and prospered; she is rich and powerful. It seems reserved for you to madly scheme for the overthrow of that which is justly considered to be the support of the Empire, i.e. its Constitution—stem and branches. For you your country's evil destiny has begotten—' Self Government' and ' Home Rule.' This generation and that to come are condemned to watch your and your disciples' attempts at the ' disintegration of the State into Joint Stock Companies,' ruled by a ' Board of Directors,' duly elected, it may be ; but their character and aim having much in common with those of ordinary mining company directors.

It is true the Witans and the Witenagemote were not exactly the parliaments of our times; there was no Committee Room Number Fifteen. And the former certainly did not resemble the gatherings at 'Spring Gardens.' Yet the Witenagemote was a great meeting for the making of laws and the voting of taxes. It was an assembly of the wise of the realm, and though the members were bishops, earldormen, thanes, magistrates of boroughs, four-men, reeves of townships, you may say, more or less aristocrats and optimats; the Witenagemote represented the whole English people, as the wise moots of each kingdom represented the several peoples of each. In all, the freemen and citizens gathered round the wise men at London and Winchester, and participated by acclamation in the election of a king.

But what about the Constitution, the government under the Normans?

Sir, you know it proceeded on Saxon principles. These ancestors of your Nation had the Grand Council of the lords and wise men. They had the King, 'who reserved to himself from the freemen nothing but their *free* service, as their lands were granted to them in inheritance of the King by the Common Council of the whole kingdom.' Thus they had the Common Council.

Behold the balance of duties and rights between the different estates of the realm more and more clearly expressed and better defined, in due progress with the advancement of the culture of the Nation. Remark also the continuity in the manifestation of the fundamental principles of the Constitution, even such as it is in our days. Indeed, William the Conqueror's assertion of the liberty of the freeman and of the representative body of the kingdom might be taken as having been the basis of that greatest of constitutional pacts, enactments, proclamations, declarations—the Magna Charta, that wonderful people's charter, without the inspiration and sanction of which all the succeeding 'part-charters' of the constitutional liberties of the Nation would never have enlightened the world and rendered this kingdom glorious and happy.

Yet who were those that struggled for and obtained it from a licentious king? Was it your mob-democracy? Or was it the English nobility; although of an aristocratic origin, yet truly democratic, because in constant contact with and backed by the Nation? Read that charter's history.

Nothing could better exhibit the patriotic moderation of the barons, at a moment when a combination of past events and then present circumstances brought within their reach unlimited power, than 'Magna Charta.' No more perfect illustration of the English character and of the healthy and reciprocally vital interests of the three estates in the Constitution could be found than in 'Magna Charta.' 'It is the noble and singular proof of the sympathy existing at that time between the barons and the people of England, and, as it were, of the instinctive disposition for constitutional government, manifest even in one of the most unscrupulous of her kingly rulers.'

However, you point to the assumptions of the nobles under Henry VII. But in this again you take only that part of historical facts which may give some colour of truth to your insinuation. You neither give due prominence to the demoralising effects of the Wars of the Roses and the disturbing influence of the bloody struggles with France, nor do you state that although the aristocrats attempted to invade the balance of power such as the Constitution had granted to each of the estates, their assaults utterly failed, the boundaries of their respective duties and rights being too well marked even at that remote period.

As to Henry VIII. and Elizabeth. They were arbitrary against certain individuals; the Nation, the Parliament, the Constitution as a whole they respected. It is true as to Mary, had she lived longer, her probable fate might have offered a precedent to Charles I. or James II. The arrangement about her successor certainly constitutes such a precedent to the events which made William of Orange and George of Hanover kings of Great Britain.

But, sir, you are supposed to know the history of your country. With regard to the good qualities which, in their co-operation its kings and nobles and people have exhibited at many a critical moment in the course of centuries, it may be excusable that your hatred of that constitutional harmony would not for once allow you to recognise its beneficial manifestations. *Your* 'constitutional' aversion to the mixed character, though equitable principles of your country's Constitution, in which three (among almost all other nations) *antagonistic* elements are *harmoniously* blended, explains your vehement denial of its excellent qualities. Yet the predilection, yet the love of the patriots for England's parliamentary and other institutions should caution you to consider well, before you embark upon your destructive attempt at the overthrow of her several pillars. This love, though may be slumbering, has yet lived through all the many ages deep-rooted in the heart of every Briton whence nought can remove it, not even the perverting verbosity and cunning machinations of an old parliamentary intriguer. Therefore, beware! there are breakers ahead. Conjure the demon which lures you, lest you may wreck and eternally drown a life, in matters political and diplomatical fatalistically misspent, but which in concerns purely domestic has shown several good qualities that entitle you to the moralist's respectful consideration. The institutions—the Constitution of your country resembles a matchless crown of diamonds; it is pure; it is lustrous; it is of a marvellous durability: only a general conflagration can destroy it.

But your conscience and intellect shall not be burdened with further illustrations such as the Bill of Rights, the Declaration of Rights, the Habeas Corpus Act, the Act of Settlement, Mr. Fox's Press and Libel Bill. They need not be examined here. The mere fact of their existence already testifies all powerfully to the equitable justice with which the Constitution allots to each of the Estates its functions, and prevents each one from successfully encroaching upon the others.

However, you shall not be harassed any farther. It were a pity if your feelings for, and notions of right and wrong should at last lose their elasticity and your mind become enlightened by patriotism and purified by honour, that *monarchical* incentive to noble actions. You hold the championship of 'democratic' virtue, and should you not be allowed to ruin your country by experimenting whether this republican-radical-liberal virtue might not be made supreme dictator and censor in Great Britain?!

Ah, sir, well justified are your enemies who doubt whether the Common Law, both civil and criminal, the Statute Law, the complete collection of precedents of and decisions on high treason would be sufficiently efficacious, if the High Court of Parliament or any other Court in the land were called upon to try and adjudicate on such an abnormal policy of such a statesman.

FIFTH LETTER

THE RIGHT HONOURABLE AND THE HOUSE OF LORDS

To the Right Hon. W. E. Gladstone, M.P.

Sir,—You shall hear Cicero once more. It may have some restraining influence, though that influence, contending as it must with fatalistic perverseness, will naturally be small. Yet read. It is the passage in the 'Commonwealth' which follows Scipio's eloquent translation of Plato's vivid description of mob-rule; a description, aye, a prophecy so masterfully true that on perusing it one imagines one beholds the French Revolution—the spectre of the Reign of Terror rising in all its hideousness from the ruins of a betrayed State and nation. It is that passage where Scipio exclaims: 'Since these are the facts (that democracy degenerates into ochlarchy and aristocracy into oligarchy) Royalty is, in my opinion, very far preferable to the three other kinds of political constitutions. But it is in itself inferior to that which is composed of an equal mixture of the three best forms of government, united and modified by one another. I wish to establish in a commonwealth a royal and pre-eminent chief. Another portion of power should be deposited in the hands of the aristocracy. Certain things should be reserved to the judgment and wish of the multitude. This constitution, in the first place, possesses that great equality without which men cannot long maintain their freedom. Secondly, it offers a great stability, while the particular and separate and isolated forms easily fall into their contraries. So that a king is succeeded by a despot; an aristocracy by a faction; a democracy by a mob and confusion; and all these forms are frequently sacrificed to new revolutions. In this united and mixed constitution, however, similar disasters cannot happen without the greatest vices in public men. For there can be little to occasion revolution in a State in which every person is firmly established in his appropriate rank, and there are but a few modes of corruption into which we can fall.'

Does not this passage significantly apply to your case? If nought else, it is a condemnation of your policy against the House of Lords.

Sir, you attack this Upper House of Parliament incessantly. Yet it forms an important part of that united and mixed constitution, where, as has been proved, degeneration and revolution, tyranny or anarchy cannot come to pass without the greatest vices in public men. It forms part of the Constitution on which that metaphor might seem to have been written: 'As in flutes and harps and in all vocal performances, a certain unison and harmony must be preserved amid the distinctive tones, which cannot be broken or violated without offending experienced ears, and as this concord and delicious harmony is produced by the exact gradation and modulation of dissimilar notes, even so by means of the just apportionment of the highest, middle, and lower classes, the State is maintained in concord and peace by the harmonious subordination of its discordant elements. Yet, though this harmony in music corresponds to the concord in the State, the strongest and loveliest bond of security in every Commonwealth, being always accompanied by justice and equity'—although this harmonious concord is produced by your country's glorious Constitution—you aim at the destruction of its 'counterpoint.' But by your attacks you prove to the patriot the advantage of—the necessity for its existence. You appeal to the passions and vices of the masses. You hope that in a moment of suicidal fury they will destroy this counterpoint, this constitutional pillar, the House of Lords. Why, why do you bear your country such an implacable hatred?

Sir, you know the elements which make up man. You know that within him passions and their vices wage eternal war against reason and her daughters, virtue and equitable justice. It is these latter which check the all-flooding, all-devouring license of the 'animal' man. You are conscious that once they are overthrown, the passions will triumph.

What applies to man applies to states. As it is with his animal and spiritual nature so it is with the organism of nations.

The masses are the 'animal' man: impulsive, passionate, fanciful, superstitious and faithless. They are yet mankind more in its infancy. They are comparable to the fragile reed, moved, nay, twirled by the slightest breeze, if agreeable, flattering, insinuating. When roused they are like a blind giant. Once set in motion they rush forward—downward. Though their own homes stand below, though there their own destruction may await them, it matters not. They cannot stop. They cannot think. Onward they roll—downward on their fatal course. Passions drive the human ball, and soon it is like an avalanche. Quicker and quicker it is hurled, with lightning speed. And now it hangs on the brink. For once it trembles. For once it seems to tarry. But for a moment. Over it goes. It falls, and the thunders of its fall echo amongst far-off nations. But here beneath lies the mob— a human mass, dashed to pieces, crushed to atoms, and amidst it is buried the welfare, the future, the life of the Empire. Yet it matters not. Democracy, Socialism, Anarchy have conquered. The passions are glutted. Theirs is the victory. Though the masses themselves are ruined, their destruction involved the annihilation of their enemies? No, of their victims. What more? *Pereat civitas, pereat mundus, fiat libertas!* Behold the trades-unions' 'policy'!

As to the classes! They are rather the intellectual man. Although infected with faults and vices as much as the masses, yet their passions are somewhat modified by thought. The results of thought are sagacity, not unfrequently virtue. Both restrain in a not inconsiderable measure their vices. Again, sagacity and virtue inspire notions of equitable justice. These direct to some extent their actions.

It is thus evident that the masses and classes are moved by opposite instincts. At the same time it is clear that these antagonisms are not the mere effect of the inequality in their reciprocal material positions.

The masses instinctively love a state of turmoil. The classes naturally prefer order and peace. The impulse of the former clamours for absolute liberty. Each and every individual is to possess, as it were, an irresponsible power over himself, the family, the community, the State—i.e. in theory, license; in practice, anarchy and terrorism. The classes, on the contrary, recognise the necessity of having some controlling, checking, counteracting element, not only in the communal, but above all in the States-household. They feel that the masses' Home Rule all round would inevitably lead back to barbarism, or create the despotism of one more powerful than the rest. They know that without an *independent* control there cannot be any staple government.

Sir, will you deny that such an *independence* can best be secured by the prestige of illustrious ancestors—substantial means (landed lords); by the prestige of high or long trained intellectual qualifications (law lords, lord bishops and lords literati); by the prestige of exceptional deeds, which imply that their hero possesses an exceptional character (army and navy peers); finally, by men justly and judiciously ennobled for their great commercial or industrial enterprise, sagacity, energy, integrity, 'civism,' and thrift?

Indeed, though not perhaps a fertile soil for the mushroom growth of geniuses, in England the House of Lords represents this independence.

It is the safeguard for the continuity in politics and legislation. It is the safety-valve of public opinion.

You know its duties are to alter or reject any Bill on which the House of Commons is not yet in thorough earnest. It has to suspend the passage into law of any Bill on which the Nation is not yet decided. In fact, it sits almost as a Court of Review upon all the measures coming from the Lower House or from any other legislative assembly, council, corporation or body. And as with but a few exceptions these measures have previously been fully discussed before the country, in and out of Parliament, the House of Lords is best enabled to adjudicate on their merits or defects, to estimate their popularity,

F

not with a faction but with the Nation; above all, to judge of their final usefulness to the Empire.

Again, it is composed of almost homogeneous elements. In character aristocratic, it is influenced rather by 'honour.' These qualities imply that it is more compact and less open to a bribe, particularly to a social bribe, than the Lower House, composed of most heterogeneous elements, whose character, thanks to you, becomes more and more democratic, mobocratic, and whose aim is vague, ambitious. Moreover, its welfare and existence largely depend, not only on the sovereign, but in the first instance, on the prosperity of the Empire and the satisfaction of the Nation. The House of Lords, therefore, is better capable than any otherwise constituted legislative assembly to support, to manage, to direct the foreign policy of Great Britain.

Further, the difficulties of its place and office in the constitution suggest the adoption of the principle of moderation for its maxim. Montesquieu already recognised this axiom when he remarked with respect to the 'principe de l'aristocratie:' 'la modération est l'âme de ce gouvernement. J'entends celle qui est fondée sur la vertu, sur la sagesse, sur l'expérience; non pas celle qui vient d'une lâcheté et d'une paresse de l'âme.' Owing to this moderation, owing to the homogeneity of its members; owing, in most cases, to their materially independent positions; owing, in many instances, to their matured age, ripened experience and cleared understanding;—owing to these it is that the House of Lords is also not only *a Constitutional Pillar, but above all a Constitutional Pilot.*

Finally, though it is not so much a source whence many new organic laws originate, its members, unrestrained by all-absorbing business callings, can and do render to the country, to the Nation, invaluable service in committees, in Royal commissions, particularly in the Judicature, as the Imperial High Court of Appeal, thus preventing in many instances the establishment of a salaried officialdom's tyranny.

The Peers themselves are on the average comparable to the firmly-rooted oak. Their position, as it were on a promontory, forces them to act judiciously. Though there are exceptions, their manifold interests compel them to be sagacious. And history, the mentor of nations as to their life and policy, because the best record of the wisdom and folly of peoples who once were—history furnishes proofs of the Lords' efficiency. It is: their actions proclaim their independence, their deliberations give testimony of their well-examined and well-directed earnestness of purpose, their judgments are emphatically their own. Free from whims, free from fits of sentimentality, unbiassed by suddenly roused passions, regardless of the clamours of faction, without fear of the threats of the mob and its demagogues, neither eager to court favour of the Prince nor anxiously seeking the fleeting breath of popularity—thus they proceed to their inquiries, thus they form their judgment, thus they give their decisions, slow, ceremonious, pedantic it may be, but conscious, conscientious, statesmanlike. Indeed, the patriot may look with pride upon this venerable Senate, composed of men, many of whom have grown grey in the honest service of their country, in the faithful performance of the duties of their office in church, judicature, community or state, many of whom bear the wounds, the scars of battle, of victory; proud signs, noble emblems of the valour with which they vindicated the honour, the integrity of their country. The patriot may well believe that when the genius of Great Britain should for once turn

from her people, and the hordes of a[n]
enemy overflood her dominions, if no o[ne of]
these senators would with unflinching p[atriotic]
spirit remain true to their country, firm in their
principles. And future historians might speak
of them as Livius did of the conduct of those
Roman 'senes' in the presence of Brennus and
his Gauls: '*Expectabant adventum hostium obstinato ad mortem animo.* Qui eorum curules
gesserant magistratus, ut in fortunæ pristinæ
honorumque aut virtutis insignibus morerentur
.... eburneis sellis sedere .... Galli sine
ira .... ingressi postero die urbem patente
Collina porta in Forum perveniunt .... adeo
haud secus quam venerabundi intuebantur in
ædium vestibulis sedentes viros præter ornatum
habitumque humano augustiorem, majestate
etiam, quam vultus gravitasque oris præ se
ferebat, simillimos Diis.'

Sir, you yourself testify to this their efficiency. Your career is a proof of the necessity
of their existence. By your appeals to instinct
and passions, by your inflammatory addresses to
prejudice, envy and superstitious simplicity,
you show that the House of Lords is the breakwater against which the all-comprising licence
of the masses vainly beats.

Indeed, it is the Lords who prevent the truism of Montalembert—' Quand le Gouvernement est dans la rue, il passe tout naturellement à la caserne'—from becoming applicable to England. The Nation must be convinced that as long as they exist the Empire will be secure. The People must know that the downfall of the Upper House would not only involve the destruction of the Lower House, but be followed both by a political and economical, social and moral deluge. England cannot but be aware that after the annihilation of the First Chamber there would be no longer a reward for noble and magnanimous actions, for heroic or intellectual deeds, nor any longer a recompense for long, faithful and successful services to community, to State, to mankind. Nay, the patriots need not demonstrate that any such violation of the Constitution as the abolition of the House of Lords would be followed by a fratricidal war between the classes and masses!—no, amongst the masses themselves, after the extirpation of the classes, so that in centuries hence far-off nations and newly-forming peoples, when reading your unhappy country's history, might justly describe that chaos in Schiller's :

> Freiheit und Gleichheit hört man schallen;
>   Der ruhige Bürger greift zur Wehr.
> Die Strassen füllen sich, die Hallen,
>   Und Würgerbanden ziehn umher.
> Da werden Weiber zu Hyänen
>   Und treiben mit Entsetzen Scherz;
> Noch zuckend, mit des Panthers Zähnen
>   Zerreissen sie des Feindes Herz.
> Nichts Heiliges ist mehr, es lösen
>   Sich alle Bande frommer Scheu;
> Der Gute räumt den Platz dem Bösen,
>   Und alle Laster walten frei.

Nor could Great Britain forget that even if the most crafty, the most powerful or the most despotic of the Nation should sway the kingly, the imperial sceptre, the House of Lords would be an equally impassable barrier against the attempts at usurpation of such a king.

But, sir, all these functions, all these tremendous duties of the Upper—the controlling Chamber, on the faithful, firm and successful execution of which the very life of the Nation depends—the patriot considers as being of secondary importance where you and those resembling you are concerned. *This* it is, he holds, *this* is their veritable *raison d'être*, that if by hereditary right the rulership should be vested, or rest in the intellectually or morally and, perhaps, physically weakest of the Nation, then the House of Lords would be, and is an equally insurmountable barrier against the usurpation, the tyranny, the outrages of the Minister appointed to such a 'nominal' king.

The failures of former 'ministerial' attempts at encroachment on the privileges of the sovereign and the rights of the Nation prove it. Sir Robert Peel and you experienced it. Hence your hatred.

You know it is the Lords who prevent the possibility of a 'demagogue major-domo' or 'Lord High Steward.' You know it is they who heroically combat the worst—a 'modernised' revival of this despotism justly called the consummation of times barbaric, superstitious and fanatic; of times when the utterances of an arrogant, ignorant priesthood were law over life and death; of feudal times when physical force triumphed, so that 'might was right.' You know it is only by their fall that this worst of tyrannies might become real; worst, on account of its irresponsibility to ethics and reason; worst, because of its responsibility towards the liberal, radical, democratical, communistic and anarchistic, but above all spasmodical mobocracy. You know that only after their annihilation it might come to pass: Here, the unfortunate king or queen, a mere puppet under the prime minister major-domo; there, the prime minister major-domus directing the bacchanals of the mob, beneath them their victim, the sacrificed Nation on the brink of destruction. Therefore your attacks.

Indeed, sir, such and no other must be the cause of your hatred.

It is not, it cannot be the hereditary principle to which you take so violent an objection. 'Lawless Lords' it is true, may become, in virtue of their hereditary peerage, lawful legislators. But wherever wheat grows, there tares will crop up, and though there *are* some 'stray' lords, still the majority of the members of the Upper Chamber are worthy of the inheritance of their, in most cases, illustrious ancestors. Moreover, you yourself have marked every entrance into and exit from office by a multifarious creation of peers. Shall the Nation infer from your attacks now that these objects of your bounty were not useful and advantageous additions to her Senate? Shall the Nation believe that they are part of the poisonous lymph with which you inoculated the Legislative, especially the House of Lords, in the hope that thus it would become infected, and thence bring destruction over the whole body politic?

Again, your leaning towards Radicalism, your coquetting with the mob, your unlimited ambition imply that you do not desire the predominance of the 'bourgeoisie.' Your career suggests that not in vain have you studied Cicero's ' nec ulla deformior species est civitatis quam illa in qua opulentissimi optimi putantur.' Indeed, your autocratic instinct must naturally be averse to the political dictatorship of building society directors, mining company directors, publishers of money and society papers, of brokers, bankers, financial upstarts and social mushroom-parvenues. And yet you scheme for the overthrow of the only barrier against their arrogance and usurpation!

This is strange, it is full of mystery; this your contradictory conduct is only explainable by the implacable hatred which you bear your country.

Ah, sir, with you it is not a question of reform; ruin is your aim and you pursue it without swerving. Though attempts to introduce into the House of Lords the system of so-called ' life-peers ' have been made repeatedly, in your time, as recently as 1856; though yours were a power and opportunity as Fate and the Nation seldom grant to a statesman, you could never sum up courage to propound such a project of reform. Much as the resistance of the Lords against such innovation must prick your indignation, much as the prospect of swamping them must inspire your expectations, much as the exaltation of a possible triumph over them must goad you on to frame and pass a Bill, the provisions of which would inflict upon your adversaries this most hateful reform—you recoil like one stung by a snake. It is: you mean their ruin. It is: your deadly instinct tells you that any such innovation might infuse the House of Lords with new vigour, with new life. Their destruction, however, is your panacea.

And yet it is said that 'even the most violent reformer will on reflection feel the value of the Upper House.'

Only tyrants or debased fanatics can deny it. Its necessity in a well-organised state is recognised. History proves it. The catastrophes which befell nations who were without that constitutional pillar demonstrate it. Yet you disregard this greatest of lessons for which many a people has perished. Why? Do you think the institutions of your country already so rotten? Do you think them incapable of the further government of your unhappy country? If so, how is it then that you believe in the Commoners? Behold, you, a Statesman, put your faith upon the mob and doubt the Peers of Great Britain!

Yet, sir, you know the first condition above all others in the organisation of a dual Legislative is, that the Upper House *be not a duplicate of the Lower House*. If the former is elective, it must be chosen by a limited and more opulent body of electors than that which elects the members of the latter. Is the House of Lords such a mere duplicate of the House of Commons? No, you know that it is better constituted, far better than a First Chamber, formed, however scrupulously, on the 'no-duplicate' principle. For you are aware that the First Chamber, the Legislative of a State, even though it be thus organised, is, owing to the elective feature in its constitution, not yet quite secured from the quakes of popular commotions, from the tyranny of coteries, from the usurpation of princely or mobocratic agitators. You are conscious that it is wanting one element, the most powerful element, the *principle of independence*: in that a seat in the Upper House is inalienable, and its holder irremovable except according to the law of the country, if and when he should violate the law of the country. This principle, however, is the House of Lords' very own. Therefore, how far above any other first Chamber does it tower?

That Great Britain's Upper House might be somewhat reformed the Nation may grant you; though French or American Senates should not be imitated in pursuance of such an aim. The Herrenhaus of Prussia, the Reichsraethe of Bavaria and Austria, in fact even your country's Privy Council might in several points furnish models for the improvement of the Upper Chamber. But notwithstanding, the Constitution of England, of Great Britain, of the British Empire, as personified in *the Lords* and Commoners, is still *the* Constitution of modern civilisation.

'That division of the Parliament into Two Houses—it was foreshadowed in the distinction drawn by "John's Charter," between the great barons and inferior tenants in chief, and the nature of the division which took place when the Parliament was constituted by the addition of Borough members, has been momentous for the liberty of England. If the representatives of the inferior military tenants in chief had been admitted to the Chamber of the Great Barons, or if they had sat apart from the burgesses, the same violent distinctions of class and caste must have grown up in England that had been so pernicious in the continental kingdoms. But in England the kings of the shire coalesced in Parliament with the Borough representatives; they became the representatives of the Commons in England; the great Barons with the Prelates were left: a separate senate—a separate order; yet not a separate caste. It is *thus* that England had and has the advantage of a nobility without being cursed with a " noblesse;" it is thus that the term " roturier " is untranslatable into English' (Sir R. Crease).

'And,' as Hallam says, ' what is most particular, that peerage confers no privilege except on its actual possessor. The sons of peers are Commoners, and totally destitute of any legal right beyond a barren pre-eminence. There is no part of our Constitution so admirable as this equality of Civil rights, this " isonomia," which the philosophers of ancient Greece only hoped to find in democratical governments. The English law confers not, it never did confer those unjust immunities from public burdens which the superior orders arrogated to themselves upon the continent. *Thus, while the privileges of the peers as hereditary legislators of a free people are incomparably more valuable and dignified in their nature, they are far less invidious in their exercise than those of any other nobility in Europe.*'

Sir, such are the Lords, the brightest and most durable jewel in the Constitution of your country—of the British Empire. The patriots and the nations abroad recognise this their irreparable and inestimable value. Amongst new peoples, perhaps in new hemispheres, the merits of their existence will be recognised many centuries long after Great Britain has become a vast, an empty desert, and the last of her citizens passed into eternity. Their enemies of to-day even admit this their valour. You yourself have borne witness to their qualities. Though meant as a threat, those words of yours uttered during the debate on the People's Bill, 'I think that they (the Conservatives) impute to the wisdom of another branch of the Legislature (the House of Lords) probable conduct such as it is not, in my opinion, honourable to that House to impute,' will stand forth in flaming letters and pronounce your own condemnation for ever.

Indeed, sir, they solemnly warn you to

'Beware of entrance to a quarrel.'

The Lords are yet a power; and they will be a power as long as the British Nation exists. Therefore, look well to it.

You summon against them the masses, you conjure the past, you call upon the hell of passions; it is true. And already they rise. But it is no longer Radicalism—Democracy that are alive. Mobocracy and Anarchism raise their hydra head. These are the monsters which your schemes have begotten. For the present the House of Lords is the object of their fury. It is too pure. It shines too bright. Hence, pereat!

But will you have power to stay the hurricane?

SIXTH LETTER

THE RIGHT HONOURABLE AND THE HOUSE OF COMMONS AND ELECTORATE

G

To the Right Hon. W. E. Gladstone, M.P.

Sir,—Already they prowl and hover around you, the jackals, the ravens and vultures of society. They descry the poisoned Body Politic doomed to death by you, whom a blinded Nation, in spite of former wounds, has chosen once more for her protector. They scent the end for which you have inflated and still inflate the electorate. They know why you attempt to rob of their franchise the proprietors and industrious patriotic citizens, whose sobriety, whose enterprise, whose intelligence, whose labours and studies have made Great Britain what she is—an Empire glorious and respected amongst foreign nations; prosperous and harmoniously developing within. They understand why you bestow this stolen franchise upon the mob, which has nothing to lose by commotions, but much to gain by them; on the mob, whose very instinct, whose very nature you well know are fluctuation, inequality, brutality, licence and revolt. The hungry senses of these shadowy birds are wide awake. *They recognise why you would fain centre the Legislature in a mobocratic House of Commons.*

Aye, like Laocoon to Illion, so the patriot seems in vain to cry to the beguiled Nation:

> . . . . O miseri, quae tanta insania, cives?
> . . . . aut ulla putatis
> Dona carere dolis *Gladstoni* ? Sic notus Ulixes ?
> . . . . Ne credite
> Quidquid id est, timete *Gladstonem* et dona ferentem.

It is as if it shall come to pass:

> Viri fatalis scandit fatalis machina muros
> Fœta armis : mediaeque minans illabitur urbi.

Yet you have arrived at the closing scene of your earthly passage when any other man in your position would grasp the last moment, the last chance, and with a final supreme effort endeavour to do at least one good action, so that he might yet hope to depart, accompanied instead of by the curses, by the blessings of his nation, and be for ever gratefully remembered as the benefactor of his country. But

> He whose life has once been tainted by
> Hypocrisy and guilt, must he not be
> For ever passion's slave ?

Macbeth spake but too truly:

> Blood will have blood . . . .
> . . . . I am in blood;

> Stept in so far, that, should I wade no more
> Returning were as tedious as go o'er.
> *Strange things I have in head, that will to hand*
> *Which must be acted, ere they can be scann'd.*

Sir, you cannot blame your enemies when they say that such might be your living epitaph. You cannot reproach them with unjustly desiring your political annihilation when they see you throw open the doors of the already affected second Chamber to the invasion of Demagogues, Socialists and Anarchists. They must feel it can be for no good purpose that you invite to the parliamentary bacchanal, so happily inaugurated by your Irish 'parliamentary' bosom friends, even the apostles of dynamite. Such a political profligacy cannot fail to corrupt the laws of the country. *A swamped Legislative will swamp the Legislature.*

You know it. You have had ample proof of the mischief and damage which may be inflicted on your unhappy country by adding to its Constitution laws and statutes for which the Nation has no need, for which the people feel no interest or sympathy, because they neither require nor understand them. And you have learnt that that which is not necessary is burdensome, hence becomes positively mischievous. Still, under your statesmanship the Empire is never out of legislative throes, constantly giving premature birth to spasmodic, contradictory, conglomerate laws.

As to the House of Commons, you do not ignore that in an assembly where various passions and interests congregate, each eager to vent its particular grievance and to realise its own special objects, the general welfare can never be considered with that patience, attention and patriotic disinterestedness, without which a Constitutional State, possessing no controlling Upper House, must perish. Experience has taught you that the Commons, composed of more or less heterogeneous elements, are liable to fluctuations. Well acquainted, as your enemies say, with the corruptive part of your country's history, you know that Ministers before you have speculated upon the tendencies and facilities for corruption which the members of the Lower House have manifested more than once. You, as an old parliamentary hand, must have observed and tried in practice that if a Secretary of State cannot enslave the Commons directly by a material bribe, he is sure to obtain their subservience by that most insidious poison—a social bribe.

The histories of Henry VIII. and Elizabeth are illustrative of this their servility. Walpole the bountiful has successfully demonstrated to his 'ministerial' epigones the venality of the average parliaments' man. The story of Cromwell and of the Parliaments from Charles I. to James II. is highly descriptive of the time-serving cowardice and arrogance of the Lower House. The Bill tacking system to Money Bills is suggestive of the pretensions and possible usurpations of the Commons, if left without a check. The details of the Middlesex and other such elections give alarming testimony of the unconstitutional high-handedness of the Lower House. The events connected with the Aylesbury election are instructive as to the tempers and tyrannical predilections which permeate its deliberations.

But is it necessary to recall the past in order that it expose the characteristics of the Commons? Your own times furnish, it seems, even better, more refined illustrations, as for instance the last vote of the Commons on the Queen's Speech.

Aye, sir, there is no finer example of their simplicity, spitefulness, narrow-mindedness and selfishness than this vote. None could be more condemnatory of your conduct, for you were their instigator.

They heard your insinuations. They saw

you draw up the death-warrant of those whose power you were eager to inherit. They watched you recording your vote for its execution. Such a sight of many-sidedness ('agent provocateur,' judge and executioner in one and the same person) could not fail to rouse their animal instincts. The prospect of political, of parliamentary, of financial, of social raids upon the body politic, upon the Nation, upon the Empire under such an abnormal leader, was too ravishing to be resisted. Thus they followed you into the lobby—though not inspired thereto by patriotism, nor guided into it by principle, but moved by personal, selfish, nay, by insidious motives. It was for the realisation of their several aims, for the fulfilment of their particularistic ambitions and gratification of their passions, for the success of their particular enterprises that the Welsh, the Irish, the Socialists, the hermaphrodite Labour Members, the Cockney Radicals, the Liberals—that all these 'representative' champions of negation and sects, of disunion and commotion, of trades-union tyranny, and priestly despotism overthrew a Ministry who at least knew how to safeguard the interests of the Nation by preserving order at home and maintaining her reputation abroad.

Sir, it is therefore not without great cause

that the patriots tremble when they think of the future of the Nation whose Statesman betrays her thus; whose Statesman, in his electoral policy, does not hesitate even to stoop to deliberate falsehood and calumny. For what else was your imputation against my Lord Salisbury, who according to you 'could not discuss redistribution with a rope round his neck?' What else was it than a wicked untruth, invented by you for a criminal end, told for the purpose of kindling the passions of hatred between the classes and masses? Upon what else than a perfidious fabrication did you base that invective, that inflammatory tirade of yours, during the County Franchise Bill agitation: 'A rope round his neck! What is the rope round his neck? It is the prospect of a large addition to the franchise! They speak as if these persons to be enfranchised were a set of wild beasts, and as if it were thought we could never have safety until they were all brought within their cages.' Yet worse! But a few years before you yourself had declared: 'Nothing could be more contemptible than a Government dealing with the subject of reform whilst excluding from the scope of its deliberation the distribution of seats, only second in importance to that of the franchise!'

In truth, it is not without the gravest reason that the Nation looks with terror upon you who in 1866 could write :—

'I do not agree in the demand either for manhood or household suffrage ;'

who, when moving the second reading of his Reform Bill in 1866, could exclaim :—

' Changes that effect sudden and extensive transfer of power are attended by great temptations to the weakness of human nature, and however high our opinion may be of the *labouring classes*, *I do not believe that it would be right to place such temptations*—as the franchise might give—*within the reach of them* ; '

yet who has since thrown the people of Great Britain in a chaotic whirlpool of reform revolutions. Posterity must stand aghast at the perverse character of a Statesman who in the prime of his manhood could write of the Radical school :—

'With this latter school (the Radical school) the removal of abuses is mainly a means to an end, and that end is a fundamental change in the character of our institutions. *Their* **aim** *is to centralise administration, to break up the masses* **of** *landed property*, to discountenance the unpaid service which among us is so closely associated with the influence of hereditary station, *to concentrate political power in the towns, to discredit the* ancient *traditions of Government*, to prevent the Church from gaining real strength and union by good laws, to make the *franchise* irresponsible, and *the representative* a delegate ; and when by these means the *sapping process* has been brought to sufficient ripeness, then to open the batteries, which until the proper time will remain judiciously masked, *against the independence of the House of Lords, the connection between religious and the civil institutions of the country*, and whatever else—of the Constitution—may still remain open to attack and worth attacking ;'

yet who has since become the great leader, the fanatic teacher of that Radical school.

Sir, indeed, your reckoning will, it must be heavy. You cannot plead that you sinned from ignorance. You know the tempers of the Commons and have tried their average understanding, and you know and have tried the electors. In fact, more than once have you worked upon the motives which inspire the councils of the former, and which influence the decisions of the latter. Yet though—you endeavour still further to develop their animal nature! It is: you understand that by this policy the remnants of intellect, character and patriotism that are yet preserved them by Great Britain's providential genius will be destroyed. For this you demoralise the electorate, that in its turn it may inflate the Commons with *the putrefying elements of street politicians and gutter demagogues.*

The great political parties, the historical parties are already broken up into small floating particles representing nothing but the passing accidents of the hour. So early as March 12, 1866, you began with the work of their destruction by cutting atwain the ties of national honour and national aspirations which until then had still bound the constituencies to their leaders, to their statesmen. There and then you struck the first deathblow to that continuity in politics, to that patriotic instinct in parties, to that true faith and self-denying allegiance to principles and dictates as to the consideration of the general advantage before the private interest, which enabled former English politicians to carry out great and beneficial reforms at home; and British diplomats successfully to establish, to consolidate, to enlarge Great Britain's imperial sphere of influence abroad. Consistent with your nature you have unswervingly pursued this fatal aim ever since. On June 26, 1884, you inflicted upon the betrayed Nation the 'People's Bill.' *Now*, you raise the axe to strike the final blow. Yet, are you sure that it will not rebound upon yourself? '*One man, One vote*' may crush the Empire; but you and yours will be buried beneath your victim.

Verily, he who can act thus against his country, he would deserve to be removed from the light of the world, so that even the shadow of his name be sunk for ever into the night of oblivion.

SEVENTH LETTER

THE RIGHT HONOURABLE—THE DIPLOMAT AND THE PATRIOT

on

FOREIGN POLICY

To the Right Hon. W. E. Gladstone, M.P.

Sir,—And yet your comet-like career excites universal interest. It is everywhere:

Ἀνδρα μοι ἔννεπε, Μοῦσα, πολύτροπον ὃς μάλα πολλὰ
Πλάγχθη ἐπεὶ Τροίης ἱερὸν πτολίεθρον ἔπερσε.

How can you explain this world-wide repute, the motives for which are so various and in their purpose hostile to each other? How do you explain that on the one side Papists and Puritan-fanatics, rebels and revolutionists, Fenians, moonlighters, and dynamitards expect from you finishing lessons in their respective moralities; whilst on the other side the patriots watch your passage horror-stricken, and implore Fate to hasten your eclipse so that the Empire be yet saved?

Sir, it is true: that you have performed great deeds, ever memorable deeds even your enemies cannot deny. Your monstrous electioneering trick, perpetrated at the Mansion House on the eve of the last General Election—your harangue on the future government of London, its duties, that is, its licence; your tragic utterances during the ever memorable Midlothian campaign; the renewed onslaught which you ventured against the House of Lords in reply to the Queen's speech, indisputably entitle you to immortality in common with a Kleon. The generosity with which you have always provided for your servitors and private secretaries will be remembered as long as there are large-hearted politicians and sycophants. The fact that for the worldly advancement of your aiders, abettors and protégés you did not stop short even at a violation of the Constitution, as amongst others, in the case of Sir Robert Collier, whom you manufactured from a two-days' Common Plea Judge into a Member of the Judicial Committee of the Privy Council, will for ever associate your name with the worst actions of the most renowned practitioners in nepotism, simonism, and favouritism. For these and other such like qualities your enemies concede, you are justly reputed, and it may be said of you that you have most consistently acted up to the maxim: 'nequidquam sapit, qui sibi non sapit—nequidquam laborat qui sibi non laborat.' And indeed, driven by the mania with which Herostratus must have been possessed, you do not hesitate even to set your country aflame. But centuries before your advent there have already been politicians and autocrats who for the gratification of their ambitions, likes and dislikes, could so far forget themselves as to sell the interests of their country to its home and foreign enemies. Yet, though they are infamously famous, yours is a fame which for ever towers above that of an Alcibiades, a Pausanias, a Catiline, an Ethelred, Dermot and Edward, a Wallenstein, a Murray and James, a Calonne and Artois. Whence, therefore, does it originate, this universal interest?

Is it that you are renowned among diplomats?

Is it that you have made the wishes of Great Britain respected in the European Concert? Is it that you have made her dicta dutifully obeyed, or at least gratefully attended to in countries for the commercial, social, political and legislative development of which your Nation not only engaged her interest and risked her property, but brought actual sacrifice in the blood of her brave soldiers and loyal colonists? Or have you conquered, won, bought or discovered new empires, new wealthy colonies, new promising dependencies, and opened new fertile territories? Have you extended the sphere of British political influence, and the markets for British industry and commerce in a manner beneficial to the tribes, to the peoples thus newly allied to civilisation, and advantageous to the Nation?

Sir, the consistency of your morbid conscience, your enemies say, must shrink before the answer, for yours is a reputation indeed, both as diplomat and patriot. Over the epochs of your country's foreign policy during which **you were at the** head of her **affairs** may be **inscribed** Dante's

> Per me si va nella città dolente,
> Per me si va nell' eterno dolore,
> Per me si **va tra** la perduta gente.

Yet it is not **to** the shades of noble Gordon that your enemies need appeal for a justification of your world-wide repute. There is more than **one** High Commissioner of **Great** Britain, of whom a faithless and pusillanimous Ministry, presided **over** by you, has made a victim for his pronounced sense of honour and bold spirit of patriotism. The fate of Sir Bartle Frere stands recorded. **The** ambiguity in the instructions to **Sir Gerald** Portal **are** full of omen.

Nor do your enemies need recall that other Midlothian campaign, when on the eve of your restitution to the Ministry you dared before the mob denounce a friendly Power, and proclaim: 'You cannot put your finger upon any part of the map and say, "Here Austria has done good."' Nay, your enemies need not repeat the abject apology you soon after addressed to the Austrian Ambassador, Count Karolyi, when a few months later, as Prime Minister, you were forced to retract those words. Sir, it has become ignominiously historic, this letter of yours: 'I will not conceal from your Excellency that grave apprehensions had been excited in my mind, lest Austria should play a part in the Balkan peninsula hostile to the freedom of the emancipated populations and to the reasonable and warranted hopes of the subjects of the Sultan. These apprehensions were founded, it is true, upon *secondary evidence*. Permit me at once to state that had I been in possession of such an assurance as I have now been able to receive I never would have uttered any one of the words which your Excellency justly describes as of a painful and wounding character. Whether it was my misfortune or my fault that I was not so supplied I will not now attempt to determine, but will at once express my sincere concern.'

Neither need your enemies revive your Don Quixotic career, when for once you yourself went as High Commissioner of Her Majesty's Derby-Cabinet to Corfu of the Ionian Islands. It was but natural, since you were concerned, that your negotiations there brought about the very decision which you had been sent to resist.

Sir, to show the perfection of your diplomatic patriotism your enemies could simply point to the support you gave to the United States of America when they complained, without ground or justification, about the application of the Foreign Enlistment Bill; to the imprecations you uttered in favour of Russia during the second epoch of the Crimea; to the speeches you made in defence of the Boers in South Africa.

To prove your diplomatic acumen and perverseness, your enemies need only mention the 'Alabama Claims.' There, they might say, you abandoned British interests for the threats and flatteries of American and Continental journalists; firstly, by conceding that the exaggerated, the 'indirect' demands of the Yankees should be retrospective; secondly, by waiving Great

Britain's claims of compensation for the Fenian raids on Canada, though British blood had been murderously spilt; thirdly, by actually imposing, instead, upon your unhappy Nation the payment to her rival of an indemnity of 3,250,000*l*.

They might also point to your vituperations of Beaconsfield, to your invectives against the occupation of *Cyprus* as a 'place d'armes' for British operations in the East; yet of the advantages of which you were the first to avail yourself in your ever-memorable Egyptian campaign.

To demonstrate the consistency of your abnormal love of peace and your diplomatic instinct, your enemies would have but to remind the Nation of your intention to arm *on the eve of the Franco-German War* twenty thousand Britishers for the defence of Belgium's integrity against French and Prussian aggression. Then turning to the following year, they would simply need to point to your conduct when Gortschakoff announced Russia's retrocession of the Black Sea Clauses of the Treaty of 1856, and all patriotic England and her friends abroad were in commotion at the portentous challenge of Russia's declaration; yet when you cowardly shrunk from endorsing my Lord Odo Russell's remark to Bismarck at Versailles : 'the situation was such that England was forced to go to war with Russia with or without allies.' And your enemies could then recall to the Nation that about fourteen years later you not only spent over 8,000,000*l.* in warfare which left

> A stream of misery and blood
> And shame upon your country's name,

but wasted another 11,000,000*l.* in preparations for a struggle more barbarous, more deadly; for a war that seemed to be the inevitable wicked fruit of your guilt in 1871; for bloody battles whereby to reinforce those very Black Sea clauses of the Treaty of 1856, and to resist Russian aggressions which your cowardice and obsequiousness had encouraged, and which now threatened no longer merely Turkey, but your country's Indian Empire.

Yet, sir, your enemies refrain from impeaching you for these acts. They know it is for your diplomacy towards races, towards peoples to whom Great Britain had pledged her faith and support, that your name excites universal consternation. They know you are famous for the abnormal fact that you, the human author of the 'Letters from Naples' and of 'Bulgarian Horrors,' could during the North American Civil War utter wishes for the success of the Southern States over the armies of the North, whose soldiers were not only kin of your kin, but champions of that great cause for which a Chatham, a Pitt, a Wilberforce had fought and spent their noble lives, for the consummation of which the Nation had sacrificed millions of her earnings—for the abolition of slavery.

Aye, once in times eternal, your enemies are confident, the cry will be raised before you: 'Where are Poland and Denmark, where are the Transvaal and Afghanistan, where is Egypt, and, perhaps, where Uganda?' Then, they are sure, you will be confounded with your defence of the Crimean War, 'so justifiable upon the ground that the danger of the encroachments upon, and the absorption of Turkey by Russia, was one calculated to bring upon Europe evils none the less formidable than those already existing, and which, threatening the liberties, peace and privileges of all, they were called upon to resist with all the means in their power.'

Then and there you will be confounded with your denunciation of this very war, at a moment when all seemed lost, and nothing but the supreme patriotism of her citizens could save Great Britain from ruin; yet when you counselled the suicidal policy of surrender. Be sure it will stand up against you, this denunciation of the Crimean Campaign, as being 'immoral, unchristian and inhuman;' for was it not you who on its eve had boasted in Manchester and elsewhere, 'I really don't think that England has often been better prepared than she is at this moment;' for was it not you who had been *its purveyor*. Your declaration, it will rebound upon you, that if England thought more of her honour and right than of the doctrines of the 'Manchester School,' 'she would tempt the justice of Him in whose hands was the fate of armies to launch upon her His wrath.' Indeed, then and there you will hear again Sir Edward Bulwer Lytton's scathing condemnation:—'When Mr. Gladstone was dwelling in a Christian spirit that moved them all, on the gallant blood which had been shed by England, did it ever occur to him that all the while he was speaking, this one question was forcing itself upon the British mind: "And shall all this blood have been shed in vain?"' Then and there you will be confronted with the indictment of my Lord Palmerston:—' But it must, indeed, be a grave reason which could induce a man who had been a party with Her Majesty's Government to this line of policy, who had after full and perhaps unexampled deliberation sanctioned its commencement, who, having concurred after that full and mature deliberation, had also joined in calling upon the country for great sacrifices in order to continue it, and who had, up to a very recent period, assented to all the measures that had been proposed for its continuance—I say it must, indeed, be a grave reason which could induce a man who had so acted, utterly to change his opinions, and to declare that the war to which he himself was a party, was unnecessary, impolitic, and unjust; to exaggerate the resources of the enemy, and set before the country all the imaginary disasters with which his fancy could furnish his speech; and to magnify and exaggerate the force of the enemy and the difficulties of our own position.'

Aye, sir, your enemies and the patriots are confident that in those awful moments of judgment the scroll of the impeachment for your foreign policy will be fully unrolled. They will hear you arraigned for the burning of Alexandria and the slaughter of the deserted garrisons of Sinkat, Tokar, Kassala and Khartum. They will hear your condemnation for having betrayed your country in proclaiming, when the proposition was brought forth to purchase the Egyptian tribute: 'I object to our making Turkey a victim to *the insatiable maw of these stage-playing British interests*. And I think we should decline to bid during the lifetime of the Turk for this portion of his clothes.' They will base the plea for your condemnation upon your friendship towards Russia and hostility against the Porte, a perverseness of feeling which could induce you not only to attack the British armed intervention in favour of Turkey against her vassal Egypt in 1840, but to strive to inflame the populations of India against Great Britain at a time when her bitterest foe, the Czar, was aiming a death-blow at the Ottoman Empire. And these three statements of yours will be written side by side upon your sentence:

| In distant and, to her children, ungenial climes, in lands of usage, tongue, religion wholly alien, the flower of India's youth are to bleed and to die for us, and she will have no part but to suffer. | There is a necessity for regulating the distribution of power in Europe where there is a certain absorption of power by one of the great potentates, which would follow the fall of the Ottoman Empire, which | From the British armed intervention in 1840, may be traced the English interest-policy in Turkish existence. It grew with rapidity fostered by the rather womanish suspicions and alarms on behalf of |

and obey. They will be pariah forces of our wars to whom every high reward of valour is denied, every avenue of hope for eminence and fame jealously and irremediably closed. would be dangerous to the peace of the world; it is the duty of England, at whatever cost, to set itself against such a result. India, of which Russia became gradually the object.

Ah, sir, indeed, not without reason is yours a world-wide repute. Your foreign policy has been the curse of your unhappy country from the moment when you supported Russia's claims for the Protectorate over the Greek Church in Turkey to the ever-shameful desertion of Candahar in spite of the defeat of Ayoob Khan and General Roberts's brilliant march from Cabul. Truly, this ever-treacherous abandonment of Afghanistan, the Glacis of Hindustan, whose Ameer you drove into rebellion against Great Britain by meeting his appeals for British help against Russian encroachment with the sneer that the apprehension of such an attack was 'nothing but an old wife's fable;' it will crush you on the day of your trial. But woe to the Nation! The curse of your temporising diplomacy in Central Asia, of your meddlesome policy in Europe, here bullying, there peevishly curbing; again, here pledging England's faith and support, whilst there cowardly betraying her interests and most solemn pledges of honour, — this curse will fall doubly heavy upon the innocent generations to come. Other 'Angra Pequenas,' other 'New Guineas' must crop up, and the precedents of humiliation, cowardice and shame which you have set, will be then used against your country.

Indeed, *Greater Britain—the Empire—has been for you a contemptible myth.*

With the rapid increase of the population in the United Kingdom before you; with the daily growing difficulties in the industrial and labour market surging higher and higher around the State barque; with the speedy development of the Colonies and the eager competition of foreign nations under your immediate notice—you have wasted Great Britain's energies in hunting with discontented or actually rebellious fragments of other States after phantoms, such as brotherhoods of peoples and sacred rights of nationalities. With evidence before you which should make you apprehensive that the protectionist policy of European and American governments might some day prevent British manufactures and commerce from entering their territories, thus entirely throwing your country upon its colonies:—you have, instead of drawing by postal reforms, by legislative enactments, by constitutional enlargements, by tariff diplomacy these British dependencies and Colonies closer to the mother country; endeavoured to sow between them the seed of distrust; you have schemed how to widen instead of overbridging any gulf that might separate the Briton in foreign parts from the Briton at home. 'Acting against all your outspoken opinions or the lessons you must have learnt under Sir Robert Peel, you have without scruple generously accepted the "Manchester" theories in vogue as to the undesirability of extending colonial influence which, it was the fashion to assume, your country had not the means of defending.' With the consistency of a morbid conscience you have since faithfully adhered to these pernicious doctrines, and England has been writhing under its bane.

Sir, can you thus wonder why the patriots cry 'Woe to the generations to come!'?

It is true, you yourself have already reaped part of the fruits of your labours. You have caused or waged wars with profuse bloodshed in various regions of the earth, yet not with credit to Great Britain's Government. 'You have tarnished the nation's honour, lowered the national character, and injured the national interests.' But England *to come* will have to bear the *main brunt* of your shame. The 'Penjdeh-' inheritance; the 'Pamirs' difficulty; the Oriental, the Russian-Anglo-Indian Question—hers will be the tremendous task—if possible—to solve. But then '*Batoum*' will be no longer a free port, and '*Kars*' is Russian. As to Persia: '*Merv*' is already connected with the *Caucasus* by a strategical railway.

Sir, Verily, your world-wide repute, where the undoing of Empires is concerned, seems more than justifiable.

EIGHTH LETTER

THE RIGHT HONOURABLE AND
SOCIAL PROBLEMS

To the Right Hon. W. E. Gladstone, M.P.

Sir,—However, when the patriot turns to the record of your legislative labours for the moral, the social and economical development of the Nation, how little he finds *there* that entitles you to grateful remembrance. And yet, the so-called 'Social Legislation,'— is it not the greatest problem of the greatest, the most stormy of centuries, the Nineteenth, a century which, inaugurated by a Napoleon, contains the life of a Bismarck, and closes with your eclipse?

What mighty events within this one epoch! Revolution begetting revolution. The different peoples, the various states, so many boiling, ever-working volcanoes. The old order of society falling to pieces. The castes swept away by the irresistible, inevitable march of a new era. The people rising to the surface.

But still more, what portentous changes are foreshadowed by this century! For, in spite of those events and evolutions, the world as yet in a state of chaos, and mankind tossed to and fro by the awful doubt as to whether the haven is close to, or whether in the future—though maybe still dim and distant future—lurks final destruction!

Above all, what a difference between you and those other two human phenomena of the great age! Napoleon, though the destroyer of kingdoms and the war-scourge of his country, still Napoleon: the lawgiver and administrator of France, leaving behind him the five codes, an everlasting landmark of civilisation. Bismarck, though in his dotage assailing the citadel of German unity, the glorious result of fifty years of duty and patriotism, still Bismarck: the pioneer of social, economical and financial reform; the Bismarck of the 'Social-Politik,' of the 'Unfall,' 'Krankheit,' 'Invalidität,' and 'Altersversicherung'! Whereas, you? . . .

Sir, your enemies think that you have been, instead of a pilot and reformer, a wrecker of this great century of genesis, so far as England is concerned. They hold that your conduct is the more blamable, nay, treacherous, because in 1866 already you had proclaimed 'Are not the people our flesh and blood?' and a little later on, 'Time is (on my) on our side. The great social forces which move onwards in their might and majesty, and which the tumult of our debates does not for a moment impede or disturb—those great social forces, they are on our side.' Your enemies maintain that, though with all those hosts of electors gathering round your banner, lured thither by vague, gigantic promises and prophecies—the conditions of the labour and commercial world; the moral and material status of the people have under each of your successive governments not only not improved, but, *in spite of Radical pressure*, become more and more neglected. As evidence of how little you have done for the working classes, for agriculturists and industrials, compared with your opportunities and with the achievements of the Tories, your enemies point to the record of the respective parliamentary labours during the last ten years :—

HERE *CONSERVATIVE*:	THERE *GLADSTONIAN*:
FIRST SESSION, 1886.	FIRST SESSION, 1880.
Amendment of the Prisons Act, 1877, so far as regarded the superannuation of Prison Officers.	Act to extend and regulate the liability of employers to make compensation for personal injuries suffered by workmen in their service.
Amendment of the laws of bankruptcy so far as related to	Amendment of the law as to

agricultural labourers' wages. (Priority of wages of yearly labourers.)

Amendment of the Mines Regulation Act, 1872.

Act to limit the hours of labour of children and young persons in shops.

SECOND SESSION, 1887.

Amendment of the provisions of Merchant Shipping (fishing boats) Acts.

Act to remove the disabilities of the police to vote at Parliamentary elections.

Amendment of the Metropolis Management Acts (Battersea and Westminster).

Act to provide for the fencing of Quarries.

Act to limit the powers of Water Companies to cut off the tenant's water supply where the rate is paid by the landlord.

Act to amend the Public Libraries Act.

Act to promote compensation to the occupiers of allotments and cottage gardens for crops left in the ground at the end of their tenancies.

Act to consolidate and amend the law relating to fraudulent marks on merchandise.

Extension of certain provisions of the Metropolitan Open Spaces Acts, 1877 and 1881, with amendments to sanitary districts throughout England

the payment of wages and rating of merchant seamen.

Amendment of the Savings Bank Acts.

Amendment of the law on the payment of wages and rating of merchant seamen.

SECOND SESSION, 1881.

Amendment of the Metropolitan Open Spaces Act, 1877.

Act to consolidate the Alkali Acts and to make further provision for regulating Alkali and certain other works in which noxious and offensive gases are evolved.

Act to extend the Superannuation Amendment Act, 1873, to certain persons admitted into subordinate situations in the department of the Postmaster-General and the Commissioners of Her Majesty's Works and Public Buildings.

Wales, and Ireland, and for other purposes.

Act for the transfer to the Metropolitan Board of Works of the maintenance of certain public parks and works in the Metropolis.

Amendment of the Acts relating to Savings Banks and to the purchase of small Government annuities, and to assessing payments of money after death.

Act to amend and extend the law relating to truck.

Act to facilitate provision of allotments for the labouring classes.

Act to amend the Friendly Societies Act.

Act to consolidate and amend the Coal Mines Acts, 1872 and 1886, and the Stratified Ironstone Mines (Gunpowder) Act, 1881.

Third Session, 1888.

Act for facilitating the proceedings of the Commissioners appointed to inquire into the working of the Metropolitan Board of Works.

Amendment of the law of distress for rent.

Amendment of the Factory and Workshops Act, 1878.

Amendment of the law with respect to the appliances to be carried by British merchant ships for saving life at sea.

Act to consolidate the law

Third Session, 1882.

Act to make better provision for inquiries with regard to boiler explosions.

Amendment of the Baths and Washhouses Acts.

Extension of the Acts relating to the purchase of small Government annuities.

Amendment of the Artisans' and Labourers' Dwellings Acts.

Amendment of the Divided Parishes and Poor Law Amendment Act, 1876.

relating to excise licenses for hawkers.

Act to continue the Employers' Liability Act, 1880.

Act to amend the Friendly Societies Act, 1875, with reference to certain societies then subject to provisions of section thirty of that Act.

Local Government Act.

FOURTH SESSION, 1889.

Amendment of the Public Libraries Act, 1855.

Act to Regulate the Sale of Horseflesh for Human Food.

Act to abolish any duties on coals leviable by the Corporation of London.

Amendment of the Friendly Societies Acts.

Act to repeal certain statutes relating to master and servant in particular manufactures, which had ceased to be put in force or had become unnecessary by the enactment of subsequent statutes.

Act establishing a Board of Agriculture for Great Britain.

Act for the prevention of cruelty to, and better protection of children.

Amendment of the Merchant Shipping Act, 1854, and the Acts amending the same.

Amendment of the law respecting children in workhouses.

Act to make provision for Extension of Allotments (England).

FOURTH SESSION, 1883.

Act prohibiting the payment of wages to workmen in public-houses, &c.

Act providing for the better application and management of parochial charities in London.

Amendment of the Merchant Shipping Acts, 1854 to 1880, with respect to fishing vessels and apprenticeship to the sea-fishing service.

Amendment of the laws on certain factories and workshops.

Acts for amending the laws relating to Agricultural Holdings in England and Scotland.

the regulation of cotton cloth factories.

Act to remove doubts as to the power of the Local Government Board to make regulations respecting cholera.

Act to facilitate the provisions of technical instruction.

FIFTH SESSION, 1890.

Amendment of the Merchant Shipping Acts relating to load-line.

Amendment of the Open Spaces Acts.

Act to facilitate gifts of land for dwellings for the working classes in populous places.

Amendment of the law relating to the grant of superannuation allowances and gratuities to certain workmen in the manufacturing and store establishments of the War Department.

Act to prevent the spread of infectious diseases.

Act to amend the Boiler Explosions Act, 1882.

Act to make provision respecting the pensions, allowances, and gratuities of police constables in England and Wales, and their widows and children.

Amendment of the law with respect to compensation due to tenants on land under mortgage.

Amendment of the Metro-

FIFTH SESSION, 1884.

Amendment of the Public Libraries Acts.

Amendment of the Building Societies Act, 1874.

Act to extend the Franchise.

Act settling the redistribution of seats.

polis Management Acts so far as they apply to sewers.

Amendment of the Public Libraries (England) Acts.

Act to consolidate and amend the Acts relating to artisans' and labourers' dwellings and housing of the working classes.

SIXTH SESSION, 1890-91.

Amendment of the law respecting technical instruction.

Amendment of the Merchandise Marks Act.

Act to extend to Army Schools the benefit of certain educational endowments.

Amendment of the law relating to Savings Banks.

Act enabling urban authorities to provide and maintain museums and gymnasiums.

Act to assist managers of Reformatory and industrial schools in advantageously launching into useful careers the children under their charge.

Amendment of the laws relating to the rating of allotments for sanitary purposes (Allotment Rating Exemption).

Act to facilitate the acquisition of ranges by Volunteer corps and others.

Act to make further provision for assisting education in public elementary schools in England and Wales. (FREE EDUCATION.)

Act to facilitate the transfer

SIXTH SESSION, 1885.

Extension of the hours of polling at Parliamentary and municipal elections.

Act preventing medical relief disqualifying a person from voting.

Amendment of the Metropolitan Police Staff Superannuation Act, 1875.

Amendment of the laws on the dwellings of the working classes.

Act for the Preservation of the river Thames above Teddington Lock for purposes of public recreation.

of schools of science and art to local authorities.

Amendment of the laws relating to factories and workshops (sanitary provisions, provisions to secure safety, limiting the period of employment, and stipulating certain conditions of employment).

Labour Commission and Parliamentary Committees on the hours of labour of railway servants.

Finally, the establishment of a State Department of Agriculture.

Sir, this record seems to justify the accusation of your enemies, that you have betrayed your constituencies, the people, the Nation. It shows that Poor Law; the Extension of 'Insurance of working men against accidents' to *all* Artisans, Labourers and Servants, male and female; Old Age Pensions; Factory and Workshops Regulations as to Women and Children; the Hours of a normal Labour-Day; *Railway,* Post and Telegraph Reforms; *Agricultural* and Commercial Legislation; Reorganisation of the Judicature, and Simplification of the Procedure in Courts of Justice; Amendment and Codification of the Civil and Criminal Law; that these are regions into which, as if it were hallowed ground, you have scarcely ventured. As to legislation for the improvement and extension of Education—primary, *middle-grade*, university— of technical Education so needful of reform, so important and urgent because of the rapidly increasing, better endowed foreign competition; there, your enemies contend, coming ages will vainly seek for your pioneering traces. Concerning the Land Question, the Drink Traffic, Prostitution and Usury, a solution of which is of paramount interest and consequence to the welfare of a nation in the throes of mighty changes and evolutions, and all four of which are problems that, the greater and more patriotic a statesman be, the quicker he would examine and strive to solve, if favoured by opportunities and power such as yours were— these problems, too, you have left to explode upon the unhappy coming generations of Great Britain.

Indeed, you have been true to your fatal mission, your enemies say when summing up the results of your 'Social Legislation.'

True to this, your mission, you have incessantly laboured in '*electoral politics*,' and 'enfranchised' millions of 'Britons,' the better to maintain yourself in power. It was in order to be true to this fatal mission, your enemies contend, that you studiously withheld from these electors the means morally, intellectually and materially to qualify themselves for the proper use and reasonable enjoyment of their so-called 'franchise.' Aye, your enemies declare that you thus acted not only because you were sure that yours would be the new 'social' forces, inasmuch as their awakening could be but slow, but because you calculated from this their ignorance and simplicity that any such electoral power would, instead of being a blessing, inevitably become a curse to themselves, to the Nation.

But above all in '*ecclesiastical policy*' it is, your enemies argue, where true to your fatal mission you have with undaunted energy plotted for and attempted to legislate towards disintegration, attacking,—devouring like a Moloch, one by one, the noble institutions of a '*National*' Church, yet the history of which proves her foundations to be so intergrown with the basis of the State, that the destruction of the former must break up the latter; yet the history of which proclaims in glowing language her devotion to duty, and her patriotism; yet on the bosom of whom you once had sought shelter, and which had nursed and reared you into power. Ah, from the first onslaught on her, your enemies say, you knew that moral principles alone, supported by a '*National*' Church, shall and will be able to help the people of Great Britain over the abyss of a social, a political revolution towards a social, a political re-organisation, on the brink of which, driven thither by *your* 'Social Legislation,' she is now staggering, dumbfounded, guideless, helpless, almost hopeless. Therefore, your ' ecclesiastical policy.'

Sir, can you blame the patriots for their hatred of you?

No, it is only too true; the record of your 'Social Legislation' seems one continual effort to blight the Nation. And yet, may you not be pitied? If you have been the curse of your country, has not Ireland been, is, and will be, the bane of your life, past, present and future?

NINTH LETTER

IRELAND: HER HISTORY UNDER THE PLANTAGENETS, TUDORS AND STUARTS WITH A VIEW TO HOME RULE

To the Right Hon. W. E. Gladstone, M.P.

SIR,—Ireland! That name, what feelings it must rouse within your soul! When the hour of your reckoning has come, will they not swell and form into one cry of anguish:

> Let me call back those evil days.
> Bid time return, that I may yet
> Undo my fatal scheme!?

Behold, already here, when the hand of death is upon you, your drooping, over-weary eyes must turn once more towards the map of the United Kingdom, and the demon of your conscience force then from your faltering lips your own condemnation:

> Roll up that map; no longer 'tis Great Britain.
> Woe be to me, my country I have torn asunder;
> How I leave England!

And reflected in the glowing flames of English-Irish history rekindled by you in 1868, you will stand forth a gloomy shadow, beneath which may justly be inscribed :

> Merciful heaven !
> Thou rather with thy sharp and sulphurous bolt
> Split'st the unwedgeable and gnarled oak,
> Than the soft myrtle : but man, proud man !
> Drest in a little brief authority,—
> Most ignorant of what he's most assured,
> His glassy essence,—like an angry ape,
> Plays such fantastic tricks before high heaven,
> As make the angels weep.

Yet before entering into the pernicious labyrinths of your Home Rule schemes, it will be just to you to unroll the scroll of Irish griefs and Irish sins. The enormity of your wrong can only be adequately measured by the 'enormity' of the wrong it strives—not to redress—but to perpetuate, inasmuch as :

> To persist
> In doing wrong extenuates not wrong,
> But makes it much more heavy.

HISTORY OF IRELAND

Ireland under the Plantagenets.

Sir, this history of the Emerald Isle, it is not so much a record of the reciprocal cruel deeds of the two nations, the English-Irish, as it presents the story of a land marked by the finger of Fate. For, the Irish—the English were, and are, and will be, two peoples whom nature, by their geographical positions, by the climatic conditions, by the products of their soil, supplementing each other, meant to be *one*, but whom, as it were, a conspiracy of unfortunate events, whom treachery, superstitious prejudices and untimely passions, nourished and fanned by foreign foes, drove into two hostile camps almost from the first moment that their destinies had brought them together.

What were the conditions when they met?

Ireland had sunk from a high standard of civilisation in the eighth century slowly but surely within two ages to a state of grossest immorality and lawlessness. *Its government being oligarchic, the condition of the people was very little short of slavery. Bloodshed seemed of daily occurrence. Of 200 Irish kings not more than thirty had died a natural death. As to its chieftains, they kept the peasants by their exactions in hopeless poverty; by their tyranny in constant fear. They claimed a right not only of taking from their tenants provisions for their own use at discretion, or of sojourning in their houses,* but also of quartering their soldiers upon the unhappy people. 'For the perpetual warfare of these petty chieftains had given rise to the employment of mercenary troops, partly natives, partly from Scotland, known by the uncouth names of Kernes or Gallow-glasses.' That this system, and the Oriental custom of polygamy, proved to be the scourge of Ireland, was inevitable. And these evils could not but be aggravated by the law of 'tanistry,' in virtue of which the demesne lands and dignities of chieftainship descended to the eldest and most worthy of the same blood, a source of perpetual civil quarrels. They were increased hundredfold by an extraordinary tenure, that of 'gavelkind,' by which on the decease of a proprietor, instead of an equal partition among his children, the chief of the sept made a fresh division of all the land within his district, allotting to the heirs of the deceased a portion of the integral territory along with the other members of the tribe—*a practice that produced a continual change of possession; thus precluding altogether the improvement of the soil. As to the Church, she, too,* though formerly flourishing, but having since in the surrounding degeneration become destitute of any effective organisation, *was powerless to stop the backward march* of the unhappy nation. Indeed, so far from being able to introduce order into the anarchy of the warring tribes, she shared their anarchy.

Sir, such was the condition of Ireland, presaging utter ruin for the future, when Pope Hadrian the Fourth sanctioned the 'crusade' of Henry II. into the Emerald Isle for the purpose 'of enlarging the bounds of the Church, of restraining the progress of vice, of correcting the manners of her people and of planting virtue among them.' Such was the state of civilisation of the Irish nation, when, in 1168, Dermod, King of Leinster, presented himself at the Court of Henry II., and did homage to him for the dominions from whence he had been driven by one of the endless civil wars which distracted the country.

Thus, both the unhappy condition of the country and the free homage of one of its chief kings, not only seemed to favour, but actually legitimised the reduction of Ireland under the dominion of England. Yet destiny prevented Henry II. from at once setting sail for Erin, and, *supported by the royal prestige, preparing by peaceful means the affiliation of the daughter isle to the British kingdom.* Instead, *a troop of adventurers accompanied Dermod*; Lacy,

Strongbow, Fitz Stephen became the real conquerors.

Sir, *in contemplating* the *future development of the English-Irish history this unfortunate event must constantly be remembered.* It impressed upon the conquest of Ireland that peculiar lawless character. It was the seed whence all the successive evils grew forth. 'It reveals the secret of the English government over Ireland.' It explains the apparent neglect, aye, abandonment of its authority, of its duties.

It was by dint of force that these adventurers had won the Irish soil; by dint of force alone they could hope to retain it. Reckless as they already were from former habits and dissipations, they were easily led to deem their swords better security than royal charters, than the establishment of order, the organisation of the peasantry, the propagation of true religion, the teaching of morals, the introduction of equitable laws. Without any higher aim, without any policy even, unless it be the acquisition of large territories, their position was merely that of freebooters, and could not but tend towards their and their Irish neighbours' further demoralisation.

Thus when circumstances at last enabled

Henry II. to visit the Emerald Isle it was too late; the English adventurers had already tasted of the 'sweetness' of lawless power, and the Irish felt the iron arm of the oppressor.

The 'lording' of his son John, though but for a few months, widened the gulf of misery that was fast opening between the English and Irish.

Sir, it was in vain that Henry endeavoured to raise the edifice of Irish constitution by granting charters of privileges to the chief towns, by dividing the country into counties, by appointing sheriffs and judges of assize to administer justice, by erecting in Dublin law courts. It was in vain that Magna Charta, that great charter of English liberties, was sent over to the sister isle. The 'representatives' of English 'government' over Ireland soon matched in oppression the Irish chieftains, and seemed to outrun them in profligacy and all their other vices; and lawlessness, rape, and bloodshed ruled supreme.

Though—once more, a part of the Irish applied for help, for redress to the King of England. But as before, the British Sovereigns were unable to render them assistance. It is true, by writs and proclamations they insisted upon the due observance of the laws. Yet this was all John and his successor Henry III. could do for the protection of their new subjects; the turmoil at home prevented them from obtaining submission to their royal will by force of arms.

Unhappily also—and, sir, this you ought never to lose sight of—Ireland herself was split into several divisions. The conflict between the North and South, East and West, had never ceased. The hatred amongst the various tribes, the barbarism amongst the different clans, were only intensified by their hatred of the more civilised intruders. It may be admitted *they* well deserved it.

In consequence of worse ill-usage the Irish renewed their supplications. Both Edward I. and Edward III. were ready to grant them protection; the same unconquerable oligarchy made a peaceful solution of the Irish difficulty impossible. Now the English and Irish barons vied with each other in harassing their tenants. Anarchism spread wider and wider; barbarism, if possible, took deeper and deeper root.

Under such conditions it happened that Edward Bruce landed with a Scotch force to 'help' the Irish. For once the sons of Erin seemed to rise—united. Yet, with their defeat on the bloody field of Athenree, the dream of independence and national unity vanished again. It had been but a dream: not all Ireland had marched against the host of the barons of the Pale. Moreover, could Ireland win her freedom from the English by the arms of foreigners?

Indeed, the country durst not become free. However much the British lords were to blame; although their misdeeds may have contributed to the *then* misery of the people, and certainly laid the mines which should afterwards by their explosion not only *fully* devastate the Emerald Isle, but nearly wreck Great Britain; though the Geraldines, the Fitz-Maurices, the De Courcys may be charged with having retrograded from the laws and comparative morals of England,— *they did not deprive the Irish people of religion, order, peace, freedom, and happiness*, which under their own chieftains they had never known.

In fact, the fusion of the two 'aristocracies' became more and more inevitable. The so-called Kilkenny Statute proved powerless. Nay, the Brehon or native law rapidly gained ground within the English Pale. The barons all but threw off even the semblance of allegiance to the English king. This at last stirred Richard II. He appeared in Ireland with a powerful army.

Her chieftains crowded round his throne offering homage. But when he left they and the barons returned to former lawlessness and 'independent' anarchy. On the other side, the Kilkenny Statute had done its evil work. Without improving the character of the English-Irish lords, it estranged the Irish tribes from the British crown; by its provisions they were outlawed.

Thus it came to pass that under Edward V. and Richard III. English rule over Ireland was but a mere shadow, a name.

Yet the Emerald Isle had for a considerable time served rather the purpose of rebellious invaders than of English monarchy. Was it not necessary therefore, was it not vitally important that the acquisition of Ireland became more than a word? And why could she not be affiliated with Great Britain?

Sir, *prove by the Irish history during the period of the Plantagenets that misrule and systematic oppression which now every day you impute to the English Nation and its government!* Ah, you will find that the policy of those kings was generally wise and beneficent; but the co-ordinate power of Parliament—its result: the limitations of their prerogative — obstructed more than once their purposes, and was often the screen of private tyranny and inveterate abuse. 'This incapacity of doing good as well as harm, has produced, comparatively speaking, little mischief in Great Britain, where the aristocratic element of the Constitution is neither so prominent nor so much in opposition to the general interest as it may be deemed to have been in Ireland. But it is manifestly absurd *to charge the Edwards and Henrys, or those to whom their authority was delegated at Dublin, with crimes they vainly endeavoured to chastise; much more to erect either the wild barbarians of the North, the O'Neals and O'Connors, or the degenerate Houses of Bourke and Fitzgerald into patriot assertors of their country's welfare. The laws and liberties of England were the best inheritance to which Ireland could attain;* the sovereignty of the English crown her only shield against native or foreign tyranny. *It was her calamity that these advantages were long withheld; but the blame can never fall upon the government of this island.*'

Ireland under the Tudors and Stuarts.

Sir, you know with the arrival of the Tudors the history of England-Ireland entered into a new phase.

The continuity in their policy, their more sagacious diplomacy, above all the extended powers of their prerogative could not fail to enable them better to restrain and to govern both the rebellious peers of English origin and the demoralised Irish chieftains.

It is true, under Henry VII. the old state of disorder still prevailed, if it did not change even for the worse. For in spite of the enactment of the famous Statute of Drogheda which contained such provisions as 'that to excite the Irish to war should be held to be high treason,' and 'that all statutes lately made in England should be deemed good and effectual in Ireland;' further 'that all private hostilities without the deputy's license were to be declared illegal'— the feuds of the 'Butlers and the Geraldines,' the 'De la Poers and Fitzpatricks' were as incessant after the King's departure as the slaughters amongst the Irish septs. Indeed, these feuds between the Irish clans were as bitter as their hatred of the stranger; and the lords of the Pale found it no difficult task to maintain a strife, which enabled them to pursue their own family quarrels, *among a people whose 'nature is such that for money one shall have the son to war against the father, and the father against his child.'*

Sir, with Henry VIII.'s accession to the throne, however, began really and, as much as circumstances allowed, permanently a change towards improvement in the affairs of Ireland.

Can, dare you deny the energy, the wisdom, and, generally, the justice of this king's Irish policy?

Behold, he not only at once recognised the evil of ruling the Irish people through the great Irish-English lords, but when Thomas Fitzgerald broke out into rebellion against the King's government, and began the struggle for the liberation of the Irish barons and chieftains from the English 'yoke,' as is usual in Irish revolts, with an assassination—the murder of the Archbishop of Dublin—Henry with the quickness of lightning crushed his mutiny almost in its first stage. In fact, the kernes of Wicklow and Wexford, Munster, Clare, Connaught, with the great 'Norman' House of the De Burghs; even the wild tribes of the north were soon brought back, under the King's rule, to peace and order. Within a few years from the landing of Skeffington it could be said that Henry's government extended over the length and breadth of the Emerald Isle; and one of the justices, the Lord Justice, durst justifiably boast to Cromwell: 'the King's Sessions are being kept in five shires more than formerly.'

Sir, you cannot dispute that this happy result was chiefly due to the King's firmness and energy in at once establishing the royal authority and, where needed, unswervingly enforcing it by the sword. But it was also due to his moderation, for, although never relaxing his grip on the reins of government, soon after the extirpation of the first Geraldines, he pursued a policy of conciliation, endeavouring by persuasion and good example to win over the Irish chiefs. His aim was to 'Englishise' them; then, using the traditional devotion of their tribal dependents as a means of diffusing the new civilisation of their nobles, to reform the country. And indeed, 'chieftain after chieftain was induced to accept the indenture which guaranteed him in the possession of his land

and left his authority over his tribesmen untouched on condition of a pledge of loyalty, of abstinence from illegal wars and exactions on his fellow-subjects, and of rendering a fixed tribute and service in war time to the Crown.'

And yet this policy, this wise policy failed. It was sterile, notwithstanding that both Edward VI. and Mary carried out in the main this system of conciliation in spite of the rebellion of two septs in Leinster under the former's reign, and of the act of the latter's Lord Deputy, the Earl of Sussex, which reduced the country of the O'Connors to shire-land under the names of King's and Queen's Counties. It failed, although it could justly be said at that time 'that men may quietly pass between Limerick and Tipperary without danger or other displeasure,' and that 'ploughing increaseth daily.' Sir, this promising order, this general tranquillity, they were but the lull before the storm. Ireland's evil destiny willed it that the sword should not be buried, and the unfortunate people prosper. But who conjured the demon of discord? Whose curse, what malediction was it that doomed the very firstlings of this civilising policy before they could deeply strike root the better to bring forth wholesome fruit? Was it the fault of England, the England whose kings, as you have seen, and must well admit, desired and strove to be benefactors to Ireland, or was this evil destiny a destiny shaped by the Irish themselves?

There could be no doubt that the interest of the people suggested, on the part of the sons of Erin, reciprocation of the conciliatory spirit of the English Government. The Irish could not do better than seek the British Constitution which, at least in theory, was accorded to their country, and to press with spontaneous homage round the throne of the English Sovereign. But the interest of the people and that of their chieftains was antagonistic. No matter whether of an Irish or English descent, whether of a Shane O'Neill, an Earl of Tyrone or of Desmond, the lords within the Pale, as well as the thanes without, all dreaded alike a rigorous and a conciliatory, though firm government of the English King.

Sir, *this oligarchy it was that had hitherto been the curse of the Emerald Isle; these, her 'aristocratic' enemies, were now joined by her most bitter foes, the priests, both her bane and ruin.* Indeed, there is ample evidence in the history of Queen Elizabeth's reign that the activity of the Catholic clergy, in deluding a people '*too open at all times to their counsels, aggravated the rebellious spirit of the Irish, and rendered their obedience to the law more unattainable.*'

That the event of the Reformation would not fail to fan the smouldering fire was but natural. And there can be no doubt as to the illogical conduct of Elizabeth in impressing upon a nation so prone to superstition as the sons of Erin, the dogmas and simple, though rational ceremonies of the Reformed Church. Yet will you, can you dispute that she acted in conformity with the doctrine of those times as to the Sovereign de Dei gratia, in so far 'that the religion of a people should be that of its king?' Moreover, had not Elizabeth before her eyes the endless crimes of the Inquisition; the examples of a Philip and Mary; the weird event of St. Bartholomew's Day?

Yet even so, it is a fact; at the beginning of her reign there was no religious persecution at all. The Act of Uniformity, though proclaimed, remained a dead letter. 'In the many complaints of Shane O'Neill, mostly for imaginary causes, there is not a single religious grievance mentioned.' The truth is, had it not been for the great Irish families, who by their mismanagement and dissensions were the scourge of their vassals, the Irish people could have lived in security hitherto unknown; the masses certainly were not unfriendly disposed towards the English Sovereign.

It may be admitted, before the blight of foreign intervention in and for Ireland fell for the first time upon her relations with Great Britain, the revolt of Shane O'Neill had somewhat disturbed this general feeling. But the victory of Sidney had at once won back for the unfortunate country order and peace. Indeed, the truce lasted for ten years. That it could have been for ten times ten years!

Sir, it was the curse of Papal interference, of Papal interest in Irish ascendency for the better destruction, not so much of the English in Ireland, as of the Protestant British Monarchy—which threw the Emerald Isle in the whirlpool of endless, useless, deadly revolts and wars. England—*only when the floods of Spanish, of French, of Italian invasion by the way of Ireland threatened to drown the English lion; when the Pope hurled his anathemas at her Sovereign, and sent his emissaries to poison, to assassinate her; when Jesuitic, when Dominican Catholicism saw in the Irish people a tool, a* lever for overthrowing the heretic Nation; when 2,000 papal soldiers, headed by a Legate, landed on the Irish shores and entrenched themselves in the fort of Smerwick, exciting by bulls and vituperations the sons of Erin to perpetrate on the British intruders an Irish St. Bartholomew's day—*England only then abandoned her policy of conciliation for rigorous measures—in her self-defence.* For had not the Earl of Desmond risen to hail the arrival of her arch-foes?

From that moment England was justified in whatever precautions she took for the purpose of checking the Irish. She dared no longer waste her energies in endeavours to win them for civilisation; henceforth she had to combat in the sons of Erin her most bitter, her most dangerous enemies, the more dangerous because of their constant close proximity. The attack of the Pope, and the almost unceasing revolts of the Earl of Tyrone, instigated by Rome and Spain, showed her conclusively that an Ireland free, an Ireland independent, likely to be rent by the savage feuds of its clans and chieftains, would become for all her foes abroad the 'place d'armes,' a gate of sally against her.

Sir, for this reason the colonisation of Ulster was a wise, it was a politic, a patriotic, a vitally necessary act. The Irish, conspiring with and harbouring the enemies of England, thus continually threatening her flank:—the plantation of Ulster with stalwart, doughty Britons, loyal unto death to the country which thus confided in their valour: erected an almost impregnable entrenchment against the flank of the Irish. Indeed, the subsequent history, the episode of Londonderry proved the all-importance of this colonisation; for not England's foreign enemies alone were welcomed by the sons of Erin; the tyrants of Great Britain, her bitterest foes at home found ready support there. But is it necessary to unfold the tale of James II.'s connection with Ireland, that sickening story of hypocrisy, treachery and cruel guilt, in which an English king strove to subject his brave people by the help of a Louis XIV. and of Irish savagery inflamed by Jesuitic fanaticism? Or is it necessary to recall the scenes of horror and outrage that were enacted within the sanguinary period from Charles I. to James II. No, sir, you dare not, you cannot deny it; Cromwell's masterful rule, his conquest of the Emerald Isle, yet by which, with but one exception, 'not a single Irishman was killed, unless he had been met in arms;' it is extenuated, if extenuation were needed, by the Irish rising, by the massacre in 1641, undoubtedly designed for the extirpation of the Scots and English—aye, Cromwell's retribution is more than extenuated, it was vitally necessary, it was the just punishment, in truth the too lenient chastisement for outrages such as the Irish history, the history of the world has happily not often to record, if at all; it was for massacres 'where thousands of English people perished in a few days, some of whom, though innocent, were burned on set purpose; others drowned for sport and pastime, many of whom were buried quick, and some set into the earth breast high, and there left to famish.' 'Where husbands were cut to pieces in the presence of their wives, their children's brains dashed out before their eyes; their daughters brutally violated, and driven out naked to perish, frozen in the woods.'

Sir, verily, such were the deeds of the Irish from the commencement of their history; and yet you hurl your execrations at your countrymen, the English; yet you will fling back the uncanny sons of Erin into the night of their former barbarism and savagery! Is it that thereby you hope the better to injure your country? Is it that you expect an Irish anarchy will be sure to destroy Great Britain with the aid of her foreign foes? Your enemies say that if there could still be any doubt as to the hatred you bear England, Irish history at the end of the eighteenth, and during the nineteenth centuries will for ever remove it. Indeed, *nationes possunt nihil visere pejus.*

TENTH LETTER

IRELAND UNDER THE GEORGES, UNDER WILLIAM, AND IN THE VICTORIAN ERA WITH A VIEW TO HOME RULE

To the Right Hon. W. E. Gladstone, M.P.

Sir,—For nearly a hundred years Ireland ceased to be a continual source of political danger to Great Britain. This comparative security was mainly due to her rigorous government of the sister isle. It is true, the measures taken by England for the preservation of order among the ill-starred Irish people were not such as were likely to foster love between the inhabitants of the two countries. But did the Irish deserve the favours of an unreasonable — nay, under the then circumstances, pernicious sentimentality of the Nation?

You have seen an Ireland free and independent implied the certain ruin of England, brought about by the coalition of her foreign foes with the sons of Erin. Again, a peaceful affiliation with Great Britain was rendered impossible by the jealousy both of the Irish chieftains and the descendants of the barons of the Pale. Not less were Popery and the Irish priesthood opposed to a Union betwixt the two peoples. England could not but be dangerous to them on account of her higher civilisation, and must have been loathsome for her 'heresy.' It was only natural that the clergy should look with vivid apprehension upon any possible *rapprochement* between the two countries which would have diminished, if not utterly destroyed their own political and social power, gained under the guise of sacerdotal administrations to Irish superstition. Moreover, had not history proved that when driven to despair by the savage feuds amongst themselves and the cruel oppression on the part of their chieftains, *then* the Irish people could apply to the British kings for protection; yet, as soon as there was a lull in the turmoil of clannish factions, that they immediately replied with atrocities to the friendly overtures and kindnesses bestowed upon them by the English sovereigns? Thus, *what else was left for England to do than to treat the Emerald Isle as a conquered land? Such a policy was politically wise—nay, it was her vital duty to pursue it with all energy*, though, no doubt, it may have been anything but sentimental or Gladstonian. Froude has well expressed this her necessity: only by England being deliberately determined to keep Ireland poor she might hope to prevent it from being troublesome. Also, the hardships which such a system could not fail to inflict upon the people were less burdensome than it appears now to its 'refined' critics. The peasantry of those times, thanks to their chieftains and spiritual advisers, in nature half savage, in culture and education at a very low degree, would not miss so much the comforts of an advancing civilisation.

Sir, it was part of this obligatory policy that England should lay upon Irish commerce and manufactures certain restrictions.

No doubt, Britain's prohibition of cattle exportation from Ireland dealt a severe blow to the prosperity of that ill-advised country. Nor can it be denied that the Act passed against the importation into England of wool and woollen cloth from the Emerald Isle was even the direct cause of a vast amount of poverty and distress, chiefly amongst the people in the south of Ireland. Not less iniquitous, considering the backward state of Irish agriculture, were the differential duties and the disabilities by which the English Government endeavoured to control its growth. But, though the exclusion of Ireland from the advantages of the Navigation Laws unmistakably closed to the Irish people many a source of income, if not actually of wealth, it would have been against good policy to allow them the construction and accumulation of a fleet; *to permit them to hoard up treasures which, as their antecedents evidenced, they were only too well inclined to put at the disposal of any enemy of Great Britain that might solicit their support.*

In justification of the Penal Laws or so-called 'Papist Code' there were, however, if possible, even stronger reasons to be advanced. The various massacres by the Irish, and the repeated revolts of English Jacobites and Ultramontanes, almost always, with but a few exceptions, set aflame by Jesuitic fanaticism, furnished a powerful plea for the enactment of regulations most likely to crush, as it was then thought, that hydra of discontent in its breeding-place. Above all, Catholicism itself—in its principal dogmas of faith deadly intolerant, and in its own history constantly appearing as a religious body that persecuted (and persecutes) any non-conformer to even the most insignificant of its priestly teachings not only in this world, but beyond the grave—provoked such reciprocal treatment by the outrages it committed. And, sir, what Rome, what the Vatican is, your disquisitions on 'Vaticanism' and the 'Vatican Decrees in their bearing on Civil Allegiance' sufficiently prove that you do not ignore. For is it not you who has written: '*No more cunning plot was ever devised against the freedom, the happiness, and the virtue of mankind than Romanism?*'

Now, such was the policy by which Ireland was governed, and such were the motives for that policy. If it did not bring forth much good, still it prevented at least greater evils. Moreover, not Ireland alone was dealt with in that manner. Against Scotland, too, that system was employed. It was the then current practice of the governments towards rash nations and doubtful, though all-important dependencies.

To charge England with mistrust, iniquity and cruelty, was therefore at that time utterly unfair and unjustifiable. To do so now, sir, is in a British statesman criminal, nay, most unnatural conduct. For so far from persistently prosecuting such a policy for at least a full century, Great Britain retraced her steps in spite of the historical lessons and sanguinary warnings she had received; the British Government, it resumed the lenient policy of a Henry II., an Edward III., and a Henry VIII. That the English Nation, that its ministers had been more consistent! How advantageous it would have been to England, and how beneficent to the Irish.

Sir, as it is, instead of opposing an unalterable, unswerving, energetic and prompt government to ruffianism and lawlessness, England now began rapidly to glide downward upon her fatal course of making concessions to intimidation, not of *a whole people, but from a club of turbulent, discontented demagogues and proletarians,* partly not unlike those who followed a Catiline, partly resembling the thirty tyrants of Athens.

Lord Charlemont and my Lord Rockingham were the first who, in deference to Irish factious clamours, abandoned the only true and wholesome policy of principle, firmness and fixed purpose for 'opportunism.' On them the lawless organisations and secret societies, so notorious afterwards, tried for the first time their odious system of boycotting and moonlighting—organisations, such as the 'Heart of Oak Boys' and especially the 'Whiteboys,' who, 'without any means or desire to take any steps of practical benefit to themselves, houghed cattle, levelled inclosures, broke up roads, murdered landlords and their agents, and ill-treated, many times under shocking atrocities, their wives and children.'

This pernicious policy of 'expedients' and concessions, it rapidly bore evil fruit.

In the crisis of the American struggle, when England seemed on the brink of ruin, Ireland turned on her. When France was contemplating an invasion of Great Britain, when Spain and Holland joined the former to help the Americans towards the destruction of the English, Ireland unfurled the banner of rebellion. But this time, the Irish danger came even from a worse, an unexpected quarter. It was mostly Protestant Ireland that rounded on England, and alack! once more she was weak enough to submit to threats and factious clamours. The baneful effect of this unfortunate event was

The Era of Irish Parliamentary 'Independence.'

This independence consisted in the sudden ascendency of an Irish Parliament, tyrannical, oligarchic, capricious, rapacious and iniquitous. It meant a substitution of *'parliamentary under-*

takers' and *proletarian agitators'* for the despotism of the Irish chieftains, and the 'lording' of the barons of the Pale of former times. It furnished another illustration, if proof were needed, that *'if ever there was a country unfit to govern itself, it is Ireland. A corrupt aristocracy, a ferocious commonalty, a distracted government, a divided people!'*

Comprising the representatives and nominees of a narrow-minded, egotistical and demoralised oligarchy, its members, unrestrained as they were, naturally glutted themselves with the spoils of a misguided country. Indeed, the only check to their despotism, a check which had been of some benefit, and which consisted in the connection of Ireland with England, in the subordination of its policy to the English Privy Council—the pusillanimity of my Lord Rockingham had removed upon the intimidation of the Volunteers. Thus it came to pass that for eighteen years the Irish Parliament at Stephen's Green ruled supreme, and that Ireland was independent; independent as regards political independence of England, but the Irish themselves being more than ever enslaved by a few noble families. Do not the names of the Hills, the Ponsonbys and the

Beresfords recall the O'Neills and O'Connors, the Bourkes and Fitzgeralds, the Butlers and Geraldines, the De la Poers and Fitzpatricks?

But why conjure up an awful past for the purpose of comparing its horrors with the iniquities of more recent times? The Parliament at Stephen's Green deserved only too well the early, ignominious death to which its injustice had doomed it from the first. Had it lived longer, but a few years; in its ruin it would have involved the utter ruin of the Irish people, notwithstanding that it passed several, under the then conditions, very liberal Acts in favour of the Catholic population of the country. In fact, if naught else, its insidious conduct regarding the Regency Bill proved conclusively the almost fatal danger of its existence. This was evidenced, the Nation recognised it, when the Irish impetuously claimed the Regency for the Prince of Wales, better known as George IV., against the direct resolution of both the British Houses of Parliament, the Lords and Commons. Thenceforth it could no longer be doubted that no matter whether the majority of the Irish Legislature were Catholic or Protestant, their ultimate aim, the goal of their hopes, the idol of their ambitions was complete separation.

Sir, that you could but have acted upon the lessons of English and of Irish history! You could never have lifted the veil of oblivion which time mercifully and wisely throws over the ruins of man's, of governments' evil institutions that once were, as in its gigantic march it passes by them. You would never have dared to plunge poor Ireland anew into the whirlpool of faction and perhaps civil war, and your unhappy England in commotion and endless turmoil. Having seen how in turns the clannish feuds and the tyranny of the chieftains; the English-Irish aristocrats; Jesuitism and Priesthood had lain like a blight upon the Emerald Isle—you would not attempt now to revive the curse of 'independence' for Ireland, an independence which must deliver that betrayed country into the claws of 'Walshite-Inquisition,' or to the tender mercies of plutocratic dictators and mobocratic fanatics, of proletarian 'doctrinaires,' of a clique of lawyers under the various leaderships of Healyites and Redmondites. But the beacons of history, to you they seem distorted by the night of prejudice and passions. To you applies :—

>Gefährlich ist's den Leu zu wecken,
>　Verderblich ist des Tigers Zahn ;
>Doch das Schrecklichste der Schrecken,
>　Das ist der Mensch in seinem Wahn.

A Pitt, for you in vain he has lived, suffered and died in the service of the United Kingdom. And yet, where is the people, patriotic, civilised, that remains unmoved by the history of this Statesman? Where is the people, subjected in economical or political dependence of another nation, that would not hail in him a deliverer? Aye, whilst the hurricane of faction was once more gathering over Ireland to hurl its unfortunate population into the abyss of anarchism, was not the sun of Pitt rapidly ascending on the political horizon of Great Britain, a sign of peace and goodwill? Must not the sons of Erin, blinded though they were by fanaticism, have beheld with hopeful expectation the rainbow of his reflection as it vaulted over the Emerald Isle? That he had never sunk under the inevitable irresistible march of time and nature! *Or, that the spirit of that Statesman could return once more and pass amongst the Nation! In the sight of him, a warmer, a more sincere friend than whom Ireland never had and never shall have, may be, the Briton would yet tarry to betray the Briton. Great Britain might yet be stayed in her fatal course towards disintegration, towards self-destruction by Pitt, the immortal author of*

The Act of Union.

Sir, long before the consummation of this greatest achievement of statecraft, Pitt had laid the foundations for the growth of a new Nation out of the two misguided peoples. He effected a thorough reform of the commercial and industrial legislation. He also overthrew many of the barriers of religious disabilities against which Irish Catholic discontent was surging higher and higher. Indeed, a spirit of revolt was abroad. The times were full of perils. He had to ask himself the question : Could England weather the storm with a mutinous Ireland on board ? Though aware of the failures of former policies of conciliation, Statesman as he was, he thought, by the aid of an advancing civilisation, he might once more try peaceful means, especially under auspices which in spite of the turmoil of the epoch were then more favourable than ever before. He hoped, not unreasonably, that Ireland free, that is, placed upon a footing of economical equality with Britain, might yet obey the hint of nature as to its geographical position, climate, soil and resources, and recognise that its real advantage lay in a close and friendly cooperation, in an alliance with England. He believed in a possible 'union of hearts,' begotten by the solidarity between the two peoples. Above all, his were legislative measures that neither threats nor corruption had wrung from the British Government, but which were voluntary Acts, passed in the first instance for the benefit of Ireland, which could therefore easily and justly be suspended, if the sons of Erin should use them to the detriment of the English.

Sir, you know in this, his premises were correct; his policy was sound; though the abolition of the Dublin Parliament had not yet entered into the sphere of his actions for the advantage of the sister isle. However, he should soon recognise the necessity of a complete union of Ireland with England. Events which turned the Emerald Isle into a hell, should bestir him to cut off at least *that* one source of continual agitation and danger; the infamously famous parliamentary 'independence.'

You know these events and the evils arising from them; they happened when the waves of the great revolution in France broke over her borders and rolled westward and northward. Turbulent as they were by nature, superstitious, credulous of falsehood, prone to violence, eager for change; it was to be expected that the Irish would be seized by the floods of this French revolution.

Moreover, the British Government had shown leniency, even culpable lukewarmness in repressing mobocratic outbreaks. The conspiracy of the United Irishmen with Republican France; the attempt of General Lazare Hoche to invade Great Britain by way of Ireland, were the natural answer to this British weakness, or untimely misplaced indulgence. Yet these events proved to be but the mere prelude to the storm that ravaged the Emerald Isle a few years after. They were only the murmurs of the storm which, as the months passed by, swelled into one of the most fiendish rebellions ever known, and which reached its climax when General Humbert disembarked with a French force at Killala.

Sir, the English, Great Britain, the Empire at last understood the lessons which Fate thus wrote for her with a gory hand. Notwithstanding the stubborn, the determined opposition of the '*Boroughmongers*,' the Act of Union was finally passed. *Their resistance was a sheer question of gold*; the peace and prosperity of the two countries, henceforth to be one, seemed well worth the one and a half million which the Government spent to glut their cupidity.

Can you deny it? Commerce between the two peoples was now completely freed from all and every restriction, and all trading privileges of the one country thrown open to the other; whilst the benefits of the English law were to become Irish property, the glory and prosperity of the Empire to extend their blessings to both the Irish and the English, and the taxation necessary for the maintenance of the States-household to be distributed proportionally between the two.

One project, it is true, one essential part of reform remained as yet unrealised. Both the Presbyterians and the middle, the better class of Irish Catholicism had still to be *fully* emancipated. Pitt had commenced this task. He had endeavoured to obtain for them unqualified, unlimited franchise and citizenship. His plan, however, was wrecked on the stubbornness of George III. The King, certainly not without reason, mistrusted any such measure, lest the priests, whose dangerous, aye, almost fatal power the Government had felt more than once before, should gain anew too great an ascendency which might become ruinous to England, to the Empire. Moreover, Irish Catholicism was utterly uneducated, it may be admitted partly through the fault of the British; *but to judge from the comparative low civilisation of purely Catholic countries in Europe and elsewhere, it was hardly likely to become educationally improved under Romish priest-rule.* Nor were reasons wanting for the King's apprehensions of the Presbyterians. The history of the Covenant, their overbearing factious temper in the Cromwellian era could not but provoke grave doubts in their moderation and tolerance. In fact, Pitt himself seemed in the course of events to have less and less approved of the sweeping reform in favour of Papists and Dissenters, though it was he who at one time had endeavoured to force its principles upon the King. He certainly began to question the wisdom of having thrown it on the Nation, almost as it were on a sudden. Be it too, that he had no longer the same opportunities as previously. When he was once more returned to power, he did not immediately resume the solution of that thorny question, and even if so inclined, before he had time to take up the final measure, death stayed his glorious career.

Sir, the Nation lost in him her great pilot through the turbulent, through the treacherous sea of nameless, endless Irish and Irish-English difficulties, difficulties which his statecraft had reduced to the smallest possible minimum; difficulties which you have increased since not only a hundred, but a thousandfold.

Sirrah! can you wonder if the patriots ask themselves how you will stand on the day of trial when face to face with him whose heart beat to the last for naught else than for England's, for Great Britain's, nay for Ireland's good and welfare? Sirrah, must you not tremble as to how you shall plead then and there, when confronted, before the immortal Pitt, with your Home Rule scheme that appears in the eyes of the Briton—of the nations abroad—to be an act, a proposal, a plot, revolutionary, traitorous, criminal, what! unnatural? Sirrah, how will you answer him, you—a British Statesman—who not only attempt to destroy his monumental work; you who not only betray the prayers and labours, the solemn pledges and sacrifices of centuries; but who dare to do so without cause or reason?

Indeed, without necessity, without occasion, without the least justification, in so far as the ideas of the great Pitt were not buried with his mortal remains, but, on the contrary, lived, grew and bore fruit, as it were, within one season, and worthy of the root whence they had sprung. In fact, the full emancipation of the Catholics was soon to be effected. Not that the policy against them had been a severe one in the eighteenth century. No, 'already before the middle of that age the laws against Catholic worship were virtually obsolete, and before its close the Parliament had become the most tolerant in Europe.' Catholics, politically, however, were still without the rights of *full* citizenship; at the time of the Act of Union the moment for the passing of such a measure had not yet matured. But it was maturescent. It required only a few more years for its full development. You know how rapidly these went by. Already in 1829 all the principles of such emancipation were formulated. In that year they became law. And with it was removed *the only* grievance which might have been alleged as some sort of excuse for the discontent of several sections of the Irish population, though not even the most rigorous enactments against Popery could ever palliate the crimes that in the name of religion, of religious disability, have been committed in the Emerald Isle by Jesuitism and fanaticism.

But, sir, to give here a record of all these gory acts, is it desirable? Nothing corrupts more than vice and crime; they spread like an epidemic. Already a mere mention of them works mischief. Nor need the rebellion of Robert Emmett—as usual, beginning with a murder, the assassination of Lord Kilwarden, Chief Justice of the Queen's Bench—be particularly considered here. The real point at issue, be it at once stated, is the fact that the period which elapsed from the passage of the Act of Union until the ever unhappy moment when you began to take an interest in Ireland was, considering the conditions of the country and the character of its population—an epoch of improvement, and, but for the Secret Societies, it would have been an era full of hopeful augury for the healthy development and prosperous contentment of the Emerald Isle.

It is true, and to mention it should be most interesting at the present juncture, in 1810 the Protestant Corporation of Dublin resolved unanimously to present a petition for the repeal of the Union. But it was only natural that the memory of their happy days under Irish 'independence' should bias their policy. It is true that seventeen years later, under the direction of the priesthood and the Catholic Association, with the aid of spiritual and physical intimidation, O'Connell, the Repealer and Republican, was returned a member of the County of Clare. But did not the 'emancipation' of their flock promise them the supremacy over Ireland when once more 'independent'? Thus, what do these events prove, if proof were still needed, after the previous recapitulation of Irish history? Do they not indict you, the author of two Home Rule Bills, in their cause and effect establishing the 'Irish Anarchy'? Do they not impeach you for high treason against England, the Empire; for criminal treachery against the Emerald Isle itself? Do they not stand forth as irrefutable evidence that Pitt's Act of Union, if firmly carried out, would in the course of years have struck the deathblow to the despotism of oligarchic factions, to the tyranny of lawless rabble, which for centuries had devastated the island, no matter whether they were Protestants or Catholics? For why else their factious onslaughts?

It is true there was also a famine. It ravaged the Emerald Isle in a manner no country had ever before experienced, when death, **absolute starvation of strong men and women and children were things daily and hourly to be told.** But what were its **causes?** Did they originate in the Act of Union? You know they were fivefold; yet could a single **one be traced to the Union?**

The Famine. Its Causes.

No, sir, in the first instance there was the pernicious policy of the Irish Legislature that enacted regulations for the plantation of and commerce in **corn, thereby** *forcing* Nature, which had made Ireland, with its damp climate, a country ill-adapted for the production **of any** cereal crop. Unfortunately, favoured for a time by the high war prices during the **Republican,** the Napoleon epoch, the only too eager adoption of such an economical expedient **could not fail to lead** in its turn to an unnatural multiplication of small holdings; the second **cause.** Could it be otherwise than that this again should **beget** the third cause, **in so** far that **when after the battle of** Waterloo the high war prices fell, **as** it were, on a sudden; when **the** bounty system was abandoned; when thus the cultivation of cereals, to the growth of which climate and soil were already hostile, was no longer not only not profitable, but did not furnish the means of bare subsistence—that then the peasants were driven from their holdings by sheer want, and the labourers thrown out of employment by tens of thousands?

Yet even under such conditions their material, and with it their moral and political position would again have improved under the ægis of the privileges of the Act of Union, notwithstanding that the Irish soil was henceforth turned into large tracts of pasturage and numberless potato-fields. In fact, they did somewhat improve, though as yet more *spasmodically*. But they would have done so *permanently, had it not been for the Secret Societies; the fourth cause. For it was they who actually kept Ireland within the vicious circle of evils, producing and reproducing each other. Thus, turmoil and conspiracies begetting anxiety, lawlessness, and insecurity; insecurity want of capital; want of capital producing want of employment; want of employment creating misery and turbulence; this turbulence again causing more anxiety and commercial insecurity; which insecurity naturally prevented the introduction and accumulation of capital.*

Therefore, until *security* could be given, *no capital* would be invested, hence there could be *no employment*, *such enforced idleness* begetting, in its turn, *new vices and excesses.*

To this baneful influence of the Precursor—Whiteboys—Catholic and Repeal Associations came the effects of a fifth cause: sir, the overgrowth, *the almost phenomenal, the unhealthy, the abnormal overgrowth in the population of Ireland*, an overgrowth such as no *rich* state could have borne for a length of time without great distress, far less an island in natural resources already so poor as the Emerald Isle.

Thus, the Irish, the Irish alone were mostly responsible for the famine. It was: that the curse of the Secret Societies had already devastated the island when the potato blight fell upon the unprepared, the distracted, the betrayed country.

Indeed, that cruel visitation, so far from casting any blame on Great Britain, it showed conclusively that Ireland left to herself would be, even physically, doomed to ruin.

The truth is: the Black Year, it demonstrated clearly, indisputably, that not only the famine did not originate, in its first cause, in the Act of Union, but that if the Emerald Isle had been severed from the mother isle in the hour of its trial—starvation, pestilence, vice and civil war would have effaced for ever its misguided population from the earth. And if it were not for considerations of humanity, for strategical reasons, for the express dictates of Nature that wished, by placing the two islands side by side, their two peoples to work together harmoniously and to supplement each other's deficiencies, yet so that the more rich, the more powerful, the more gifted, the more populous should take the lead in their joint pioneering march towards civilisation—there are some who would hold that those who attack you on account of your Home Rule Bills are in reality England's greatest enemies. If it were not for those reasons, there are even patriots who would call you England's truest friend, and not at all unreasonably—on the contrary, very justifiably, inasmuch as by repealing the Act of Union and creating the Irish Anarchy, you abandon the Emerald Isle to certain destruction by its own population; thus would deliver Great Britain from a danger which thanks to her opportunistic, 'conciliatory' policy, is menacing more and more her very existence.

The Famine and England.

But, as it then happened, England did not desert the daughter isle in the hour of tribulation.

Ah, you may have forgotten it! It is not surprising that the Irish caucus, the rabble and oligarchic coterie, that your aiders and abettors in the ruin of England, in the destruction of Ireland, that the band of Irish demagogues in the House of Commons, that *they* have forgotten the noble, the self-denying part Great Britain acted in that weird catastrophe! Yet history, posterity will remember how in the existence of the Act of Union your country recognised at once its moral obligation towards Ireland. They will record how, for the sake of the Union, England readily acknowledged her political relation towards the Emerald Isle. They will remember how your country gladly and energetically fulfilled its material responsibility, promptly alleviating the general misery, unswervingly endeavouring to remove its causes, a responsibility which but for the Act of Union would never have existed. Future ages must wonder how the hated, the calumniated, the persecuted, the repulsed, the 'alien' England could so strenuously exert herself to rescue the Irish from the dreadful consequences of their own wickedness. Indeed, inspired by the lofty ideas of the Act of Union, your country did not recoil from the tremendous task of feeding half the population of Ireland, over 3,000,000, an undertaking such as had never before been carried out in the world's history. The British buried the wrongs and insults and injuries they had received from the sons of Erin; every man and woman and child in the kingdom hastened to help their 'Irish brethren.' All England supported the daughter isle, though all England knew that the curse of Ireland—that the Secret Societies would repay her with rebellion, mutilation and murder. For as to Irish gratitude! All England understood that the sons of Erin, that the Irish people *durst* not be grateful; the tyranny of their demagogues prevented them. How well this is shown amongst many others, in the case of Forster, your Forster whose shades you cannot desire to encounter on the day of your trial! Behold! Forster, even he who was so conspicuous amongst those who exerted themselves in the alleviation of the distress and despair in Ireland, even he did not escape the murderous attacks of Fenians and Moonlighters. And why? Because this, his very devotion to the Irish people during the famine was a crime against the agitators. It was a crime, inasmuch as it naturally weakened the despotism of the caucus of demagogues which they exercised by spreading falsehoods against England, by terrorising Ireland. It was a crime in that it restrained them from trafficking in the misery of their countrymen. His life was held to be forfeited by the Fenians, Land Leaguers and Dynamitards, because, whilst Chief Secretary in the Emerald Isle, he strove to establish peace, and to maintain the law—the only means to make the daughter isle prosperous, and its misguided population for once contented, thus starving out the ulcer of a clique of demagogues.

Improvement of Irish Affairs.

Yet England, though her efforts were repaid with the grossest ingratitude, she had the inward satisfaction that under the ægis of the Act of Union she had nobly performed her duty and successfully.

Sir, even you who are notorious for perverting historical facts, even you would fail to dispute that in spite of those factious commotions for the Repeal of the Union, in spite of the causes which led to the calamitous event of the famine, in spite of that dreadful event itself— Ireland had improved her material affairs in the course of years. Indeed, before that cruel visitation, there was the beneficial administration of a Drummond, beneficial as to law and order, thus beneficial for the general morals. Nor could the repeal of the Navigation Laws, the admission of Ireland to all the advantages of British commerce be without salutary effects. Thus, the Emerald Isle was before the famine a decidedly improving country in respect of production, notwithstanding the traitorous actions of the secret societies. Aye, the Irish were even so far, socially, a contented people, for what else indicates the significant statement which O'Connell, the Republican and Repealer uttered at Youghal (1829): '*I recollect when we agitators were almost as much execrated by our fellow-slaves* (?) *as we* (the agitators) *were by our oppressors* (?)'

But this improvement was even more promising after the Black Year. 'Ireland advanced more rapidly, and recovered from the condition of almost total wreck more completely than any other country would have done or has ever done.' For the commutation of the tithe, the last point in the 'Catholic grievance,' then wrought the beneficial changes which had been expected from the Act. And with great truth has Lecky stated: 'The Irish Church, when it was supported by tithes, was the most unpopular ecclesiastical establishment in Europe. . . . After the commutation of tithes nearly all active hostility to it disappeared. *The Church question speedily became indifferent to the great mass of the people*; the Protestant clergy were a beneficent, and usually a popular element in Irish society, and *the measure which finally disendowed them was much more due to the exigencies of English party politics than to any genuine pressure of Irish opinion.*' Again, with the decrease of the population of Ireland, the number of acres under cultivation increased in proportion. Thus, whilst in 1841 there had been for each individual of the rural population one and eight-tenths of an acre, about twenty years after there were two and a half to three acres for each peasant. Favoured by Nature, this general improvement extended to the returns of the tillage of the soil. The potato crop, the corn crop produced in each successive year a larger quantity than in the preceding, so that in 1868 the potato harvest was estimated at 4,062,207 tons; the wheat produce at 954,818 quarters; the oats crop at 7,628,857. This general improvement was not less visible in the rise of wages. As you yourself testified in the speech by which you introduced your first Land Bill—up to the year 1860 and later on, there was a great and universal increase in the rate of wages throughout Ireland, amounting in some places to 30 per cent., in others to 50 per cent., and in some to as much as 100 per cent. This improvement included even the tenements of the Irish peasants, in so far that the third- and fourth-class houses, of which there were in 1841 491,278 and 533,297 respectively, gradually decreased, whereas the number of the first and second class increased in the same ratio.

English Land Policy *in Ireland and Fenianism.*

Sir, such was the general improvement, solely the result of the beneficent advantages which the provisions of the Act of Union had conferred upon Ireland. Sir, such was the general improvement in spite of certain factious commotions. It needs no commentary. It shows that if England had really neglected her protective policy towards the daughter isle in ages gone by, the record of this amelioration in the condition of the Irish since the Act of Union would fully palliate all her former shortcomings.

Indeed, it proves that your country has been almost too solicitous for the welfare of the Emerald Isle. Behold, being induced by party tricks, by false representations to believe that there was another grievance, the Land Question, which, unless it was settled according to the pretensions of the demagogues, would always stand hostile between the two peoples—the policy of Great Britain embarked even upon that suicidal Land Legislation, by which it not only again granted concessions to threats and violence, but by which with the connivance of a British Statesman, in fact upon his instigation, *the doctrine of spoliation and murder for political ends was raised to a moral principle in politics.* For, though *not yet fully developed by you*, already the very first Act, the Encumbered Estates Act, purporting to redress this grievance: it was an

Act of the grossest injustice; it was the seed whence all future troubles should grow.

No doubt it brought large tracts of heavily mortgaged land within the reach of the farmer in general. Yet it replaced the landlord's agent by the middleman and moneylender; it acted thus demoralisingly upon the agricultural estate itself. Instead of benefiting the poor peasant, it introduced a new, a foreign element into the class of landowners. Above all else, it hastened and intensified the commercial ruin of hundreds of old families, and resulted in their expulsion from hearth and home.

However, it is unnecessary to dwell here at great length on the proceedings of the Encumbered Estates Court or on Deasy's Act in 1860, the sequels of that first iniquitous measure in the Land Reform.

Nor need the rebellion of Smith O'Brien or the conspiracy of Mitchel be particularly mentioned here. They were the effects of that policy, vacillating and without principle, now imposing upon the country the Treason Felony Act and suspending the Habeas Corpus Act; now for the furtherance of British party politics betraying by unlimited concessions to the rabble those who loyally defended the interests of the

Empire. It was but natural that a policy such as that, founded upon what might justly be called a felony committed by a factiously biassed legislative assembly, would result in felony and renewed criminal agitation on the part of the Irish, than to whom, *next to a fair or a funeral, nothing is dearer than a conspiracy or sanguinary riot.*

Neither could the bursting of the *Sadleir and Keogh* bubble—'Sadleir and Keogh!' *the leaders of the first Irish Parliamentary clique in the House of Commons*—come as a surprise. The whole history of Ireland, from the dawn of historical records to the present day, shows only too clearly how easily the sons of Erin were led at all times by impostors and swindlers and traitors, no matter whether they appeared in the gown of a priest or Jesuitic fanatic; under the guise of a deliverer or as the apostles of dynamite.

Nor is it necessary to enlarge upon the influence which the revolutionary events that happened abroad during the next twelve years exercised upon the Irish demagogues. It would have been unnatural in at least a large section of the Irish if the July Revolution in France had not found an echo amongst them. And when the Indian Mutiny broke out, to men such as Stephens and O'Donovan Rossa, to the young members of the Phœnix Club—the Literary Phœnix Club!—it must have seemed to afford the most favourable opportunity *for establishing, upon the principles of French Anarchy and Terrorism, an Irish Republic.* The life-purpose of Fenianism being destruction, they could not fail at once to appreciate the chance of finally ruining an Empire, by that Indian Mutiny already shaken to its very foundations.

Sir, it is enough to know that Ireland was again rolling into the all-devouring vortex of faction; that once more it fell into the claws of a band of robbers and assassins, of criminals. For even you cannot deny, even you cannot pervert the fact that the Clan na Gael, the Invincibles—that Fenianism were and are such and naught else. *They represented no grievance. They did not formulate or proffer reasonable claims for consideration. They set up no ideal of patriotism. Their aim was fighting and bloodshed. The daggers of their members were raised against society indiscriminately. Revolution — animal communism—being their ideal; massacre, as the best means to realise it, was the idol whom they worshipped.* Indeed, as to that part of Irish history, it is enough to know that the general improvement in the economical affairs of Ireland was henceforth checkmated as usual in the first instance through factious violence and fiendish conspiracies.

The interesting, the momentous part in this new phase into which Irish history now enters, its weird and lamentable characteristic, this it is: that this change for the worse in the condition of Ireland is mainly due to the perverseness of a so-called British Statesman. Sir, this is the most remarkable fact in the Irish-English history of recent times, that the moonlighters, the cattle mutilators, the assassins, the dynamitards, the Land Leaguers, that the clique of Irish demagogues in the House of Commons—truly representative of the most lawless rabble—that these sprang up under your patronage. Indeed, this phenomenal feature in the new development of Irish-English history; it is all-important that it be recorded, that it be examined. The Nation, the coming generations, posterity ought to, they must learn how you not only furnished those Fenians with the means to organise against the laws of your country, but actually forged and are forging for them the very weapons wherewith to destroy Great Britain.

ELEVENTH LETTER

THE IRISH GLADSTONIAN ERA AND THE HOME RULE BILL OF 1886

To the Right Hon. W. E. Gladstone, M.P.

SIR,—On March 30, 1868, opened this new phase in the history of Ireland, which posterity may well call the Irish Gladstonian era of humiliation, surrender, affliction and treason, and which you yourself have placed under the symbol of an Upas Tree, whose branches it is your fatal mission to cut off, the better to wound the Nation and to poison the body politic. On that day was enacted the first scene in the unnatural drama: the dismemberment of the Empire—on that day was enacted the great betrayal scene between

Mr. Gladstone and the Irish Church.

Sir, can you deny it—though you knew there were numerous important matters relating to Scotland and England urgently requiring the attention of the Legislature—on March 30 you moved your famous resolutions which led to the disestablishment of the Irish twin-sister of the United Church that according to the fifth article of the Act of Union 'was to be deemed and taken to be an *essential and fundamental* part of that Union'? On that day by three resolutions you made *the first move in your campaign for the severance of the Emerald Isle from the British Isle, for the disruption of the Empire.*

It is true you then stated that, although your measure might alter some of its provisions, yet you would 'confidently contend that by it you were confirming the general purport and substance of that Act of Union.' It is likewise admitted that the State's endowment of the Church of the minority was 'equitably' indefensible, *though the burden it had imposed upon the majority had been removed; though the establishment was no longer felt since the commutation of tithes.* (Page 177.)

But the motive for the introduction of your portentous measure—it had not originated in your strong sense of justice. The Act for the Disestablishment of the Irish Church had not been suggested by considerations of equity, nor was it effected by reasons of general policy. For, whilst for twenty-five years in power you had never, not once, however feebly, raised your voice in support of redressing any Irish 'grievance.' On the contrary, as my Lord Beaconsfield taunted you, 'you had during all this time never done anything for Ireland but make speeches in favour of the Irish Church.'

Sir, this your motive, in the first instance it had sprung from party political considerations. It originated in your supreme egotism. It was the outcome of your unlimited ambition and love of power. Indeed, how well it is said by my Lord Grey, the liberal Lord Grey, '*It was not the welfare of the nation, but party interest which seems to have guided the conduct of Mr. Gladstone.* The resolutions he brought forward and the manner in which they were advocated made all compromise impossible, and in the electoral campaign when Parliament was dissolved *his speeches were calculated to inflame to the very utmost the fierce party passions of the Roman Catholics and Protestants in Ireland, and to kindle a spirit of hatred against this country in the minds of the Irish.*' In the second instance it was a concession to violence. For party purposes, for personal advantages, for selfish considerations, but *also from cowardice,* you surrendered to the events *which rapidly and naturally followed the* announcement *in February* 1867 *of the intention of the then Government once more to try in Ireland a forbearing policy, and restore to its population the Habeas Corpus Act.* It was a concession to the events *which immediately resulted therefrom :* a concession to the murder of policemen at Manchester by Fenians ; to the Irish plot to seize the arsenal at Chester ; to the Fenian atrocity at the Clerkenwell Prison, when, in broad daylight, in the midst of a crowd of mothers and their children, Irish conspirators, in the attempt to set two Fenian captives at large, placed and exploded a barrel of gunpowder, spreading mutilation and death amongst more than a hundred innocent persons. In the third instance you were goaded to that measure by fury over the success of your rival Disraeli.

These were the causes which ' *revived* ' the Irish Church Question, and brought it within the range of practical politics.

Thus, your first move towards the settlement of the Irish problem, if a problem there was, bore within itself the curse of opportunism, of selfishness, of iniquity. It proved, instead of being a gospel of peace and goodwill, to be a scourge upon the betrayed sons of Erin. It was, as my Lord Derby exclaimed, ' a measure unjust, *calculated to shake confidence in all property, and to alienate those who had hitherto been the firmest supporters of the British throne and of British connection, and to stimulate to fresh demands that portion, that violent portion of the Roman Catholic population which looks forward to ultimate emancipation from the control of the British Legislature.*' By it you sowed the seed of dragon's teeth, from which should grow forth the assassins of my Lord Cavendish and of Burke. It became—so far from being a settlement, as you and John Bright proclaimed, 'tending to a more true and solid union between Ireland and Great Britain, giving tranquillity to our people, greater strength to the realm, and adding new dignity to the Crown'—the source of all these fiendish commotions under which the Emerald Isle, under which England sold by you her 'Statesman,' have since been writhing in the agony well nigh of despair. Indeed, the curse which was inherent in that measure, it affected even the administration under your supervision of the provisions the Disestablishment Bill contained; it affected it in such a manner that Disraeli could well say, 'The law has been defeated, the Legislature baffled, the country swindled.' 'And yet, however criminal in its motive, however iniquitous in some of its principles, a just solution of this Irish Church Question might have contributed to the welfare of the Irish, of the Nation, if it had not been so dastardly used for party purposes!'

The Fruits of Mr. Gladstone's Irish Church Policy.

Sir—As it is,—at the best an act of spoliation, it was your first success in that perverse scheme of yours to throw the millions of pounds with which you have since endowed priestly tyranny, Jesuitic inquisition and Fenian terrorism, as a heavy debt upon your unhappy country. Could it thus be otherwise than that

> Once stept in guilt, once seen the worldly gain
> Of theft, of robbery, of sin,

you should now rapidly roll down your fatal course?

Could it be otherwise than that the Disestablishment Bill should be followed by the *Irish Glebe Lands Bill*, by which you would have authorised loans from the spoils of the Irish Church to assist in the purchase of glebes and the erection of glebe houses for the Irish Roman Catholic clergy, a proposal of which even Maguire, Maguire the first mover for Disestablishment, stated: that if the Government had been so mad as to introduce the Bill at the commencement of the Session, Scotland would have been up in arms against it, but as it happened, it was a *well-planned attempt to steal a march upon Great Britain?*

Was it otherwise to be expected than that, in answer to this your move 'for conciliating Irish discontent,' the Romish Irish prelates should, in 1871, issue a manifesto demanding denominational education, or 'educational equality,' as they termed it, in imitation of the phrase you used when speaking of your *Glebe Lands Bill,* as embodying the 'question of *equal* treatment of the clergy of all religions?' It was but natural that after your first lesson—that after your overture, they should clamour for the overthrow of the existing unsectarian education which *in reality placed all denominations on a footing of perfect equality. It was but natural that they should claim as their right from the national, the British, the Protestant English treasury the endowment of schools and colleges over which they alone exercised control, which were under their exclusive management, which were devoted to the teaching of Ultramontane* doctrines—*doctrines you have since denounced with horror in your dissertations* 'The Vatican Decrees in their bearing on Civil Allegiance' *and* 'Vaticanism;' *doctrines of which you have said* 'that they were an incentive to general disturbance, a premium upon European war;' *doctrines which you have characterised as* 'aiming deadly blows at the freedom of mankind.' Indeed, this policy of the Romish Catholic prelates—it was but natural: *l'appétit vient en mangeant.*

But above all, could it be otherwise than that your perverse conduct, your almost felonious actions should be followed by fresh agrarian crimes, by murders and deeds of violence; that lay and clerical agitators, that the Irish demagogues redoubled their activity in stirring the ignorant peasantry to acts of lawlessness and sedition? For apart from this raid upon the sister Church of your country, apart from that violation of the right of property, and, sir, of equity, had you not only allowed the Habeas Corpus Suspension Act to expire, but also released several of the most notorious Fenian criminals from their only too just captivity? Ah, it did produce its results, this abnormal lenity of yours, this egotistical weakness of yours, this your damnable bargaining for power with national interests which you held in trust from your country. England quivered under them. For, the first use which the Fenians, whom your opportunism had set at large, made of their freedom was to proclaim in vehement terms their unabated hostility to the British Government. They then instigated a new sanguinary agitation for procuring the release of the remaining Fenian convicts. And, before leaving for America, they did their utmost to incite anew their beguiled countrymen to open rebellion against the Crown.

But this your perverse policy begot yet something worse, your

First Land Bill.

On the 15th of February, 1870, it was when you brought forth this ever-memorable measure, by which you ' *wished to alarm none, to injure none.*' On that day you inflicted upon the Nation that kaleidoscopic proposal, the adoption of which was to bring ' *hope where there has been despondency, confidence where there has been mistrust; and by which, where there has been alienation and hate, there shall, however gradually, be woven the ties of a strong attachment between man and man!'* On that day you felled the second branch of that Upas Tree, an act of which your *hope was high and ardent that you would live to see it prosper, and that in Ireland, which you desire to unite to England and Scotland by the only enduring ties—those of free will and free affection—peace, order and a settled and cheerful industry will diffuse their blessings from year to year and from day to day over a smiling land.*

Sir, the smiling land! Through the Land Bill! Indeed, ere the year that saw its painful birth had passed away, England, the present generation, you yourself reaped

The Firstlings of this Land Bill.

That you could deny it!—the 'legalisation' of the Ulster custom henceforth throughout Ireland—compensation for improvements, and the price of the goodwill of the land to the outgoing tenant; the new rights by which the farmer could claim from the landlord damages for disturbance or eviction; the regulation that for the purpose of creating a peasant proprietary the Board of Works should advance loans at $3\frac{1}{2}$ per cent. interest for the purchase of holdings; the clause that the Court was to consider when valuing the tenant's compensation, whether the demanded rent was reasonable—all these provisions of the Land Bill, so hostile to the landlords; all these concessions so deferring to the clamours of the demagogues: they produced but a new, a more vehement, a more cruel form of terrorism. They taught the rabble how easy it would be in future to break *contracts* under a so-called 'British' Government, which itself could thus violate the first principles of ownership and virtually confiscate for the benefit of Great Britain's enemies the property of those who, whatever their shortcomings were, had at least been the staunchest, the most loyal supporters of the Law and the Crown. And the rabble recognised instinctively—at once—who and what was the man that ostensibly stood at the helm of the State ship, but who allowed her to drift out of, though a stormy, yet open and comparatively safe sea into a gulf studded with shoals and rocks, and with deadly breakers ahead. The rabble understood and responded to your purpose to wreck the State vessel, so that she should break up in mouldering fragments. The Irish demagogues organised afresh lawless bands of armed men, who swarmed over the county of Mayo, under threat of instant death coercing the farmers into taking an oath to unsettle their pasture lands. They revived the memory of O'Connell, of the 'martyred' Fenian assassins. They resumed their seditious schemes. They returned John Martin the convict to Parliament as a Home Ruler. Aye, they went forth to preach the doctrine of Separation and to proclaim the Irish Republic.

Sir, it is true you replied with THE CRIMES ACT—considering you were its author—one of the most coercive measures that has been enacted by a British Government against rebellious Ireland; though *it certainly was not only justifiable in view of the unjustifiable outrages of the agitators and their beguiled tools, but vitally necessary, and which would have operated beneficially and beneficently to the betrayed Irish people, if the Government had for a length of time persisted in a systematic administration of its provisions.* But already a few months later you fell back upon your '*opportunistic*,' your '*conciliatory*,' your '*expiatory*' policy. You released the Fenian convicts who were still in prison. And lest the mischief thus wrought might not work sufficiently detrimental to the prosperity and order of Ireland, to the welfare and peace of England, you banished them from the English, from the Irish territory; you drove them out of the supervision of the British police; you set them at large in the United States. Can you wonder if your enemies hold that by this abnormal act—abnormal in an 'experienced Statesman'—you materially contributed towards the completion of your treason-felony against the Empire—towards Separation, towards dismemberment, in so far as you became, as it were, the 'recruiting sergeant' for Great Britain's most relentless foe: for the American Fenians—the Clan-na-Gael?

Why! Indeed, you were well repaid. Your country, you yourself immediately felt the painful effects of your culpable, vacillating, compromising conduct.

When a French deputation arrived in Ireland to thank the Irish Ambulance Society for the assistance which it had rendered France during the Franco-German war; the sons of Erin expressly indulged in violent demonstrations against your country. But worse! Juries refused to convict of murder Fenians and rebels against whom not only lay the clearest circumstantial evidence, but who had been taken *in delicto flagrante*. The *Irishman*, the organ of the Nationalists, **proclaimed** *that the man who shot* an informer against moonlighters, cattle-mutilators and assassins, was, *so far from being a criminal,* a hero, *worthy of honour and reward.* At **the** same time, the agitation for Home Rule became more and more turbulent. During the election **of a** Mr. Smyth for Westmeath, it was even declared 'that in him the electors were sending a man to **Parliament** to **tell** Mr. Gladstone *his* **mock** *legislation* **was a** *humbug,* and *that the Nationalists would not stand a base, bloody and brutal Whig in Ireland.'*

And **yet, bent** upon your fatal mission, you **did not** pause in your pernicious legislation for **the 'settlement'** of Ireland. Though you saw **the** Empire shaken almost to its foundations **by the quakes of your** policy **of** destruction; bent upon your fatal mission, you raised your axe to strike off the third branch of the Upas Tree.

Truly, not without reason are you called the 'great wrecker.'

You heard the murmurs of **the** coming gale. You saw the clouds gather thicker and thicker over Ireland. *In the face of the growing turmoil, in answer to the factious clamours for Home Rule of the demagogues and Invincibles, you even declared at Aberdeen in September,* **1871:**

Why is Parliament to be broken up? Has Ireland great grievances? What is it that Ireland has demanded *from the* Imperial Parliament *and that the* Imperial Parliament *has refused?* It will not do to deal with this matter in vague and shadowy assertions. *I have* **looked** *in vain for* **the setting** *forth of* **any** *practical scheme of policy which* **the** *Imperial Parliament is not equal to deal with, or which it refuses* **to deal with,** *and which is to be brought about by Home Rule.*

You would **expect** when it is said that the Imperial Parliament is to be broken up—you would expect that at the very least **a** case should be made out, showing there were great subjects of policy and great demands necessary for the welfare of Ireland, which the representatives of Ireland had **united to ask, and which** the representatives of England, Scotland, **and Wales** had united to refuse. *There is no such grievance. There is nothing that Ireland has* asked *that* this country *and that this* **Parliament** *has refused.* This Parliament **has done for Ireland what** *it would have scrupled to* **do for** England *and for Scotland. What are the inequalities of* England *and* Ireland*? I declare that I* know none, except that there are certain taxes still remaining which **are** levied over Englishmen **and Scotchmen,** and which are not levied over Irishmen; and likewise that there **are** certain purposes for which public money is freely **and** largely given in Ireland, and **for which it** is not given in England or Scotland. *That seems to me to be a very feeble* **case indeed** *for the argument which has* **been** *made, by means of which, as we are told, the fabric of the United Parliament of this country is to be broken.*

But, although the sanguinary lessons of Irish history; though your own bitter experience must have warned you that compromise, that

'CONCILIATION,' as your bosom friend, John Morley has pointedly remarked, 'MEANS, IN PLAIN LANGUAGE, SEPARATION *where Ireland is concerned*;' though you yourself emphatically denied that there was any cause for the Irish to complain about English misrule—you now flung upon your unhappy country the

Irish University Bill,

'a measure vital not only to the honour and existence of the Government, but to the welfare of Ireland!'

Ah, sir, it is well for posterity to have your record of this University Bill. The Empire cannot yet be lost if the patriots succeed in rousing the Nation—the people to a second perusal of 'The Vatican Decrees in their bearing on Civil Allegiance.' For there it stands marked that *this Bill was the final settlement* of Ireland's grievances.

'When Parliament had passed the Church Act of 1869, and the Land Act of 1870, *there remained only under the great head of Imperial equity one serious question to be dealt with— that of higher education.* I consider that the Liberal majority of the House of Commons, and the Government to which I had the honour and satisfaction to belong, formally tendered payment in full of this portion of the debt by the Irish University Bill of February, 1873. Some, indeed, say *that it was overpaid.*'

However, in justice to you, it must be stated, the blow was stayed. The Bill which '*nobody wanted, nobody accepted; which settled nothing,* BUT UNSETTLED EVERYTHING:' on March 12 it was rejected by the patriotism and common sense of the Nation.

But the event, the lamentable event of its appearance, left its traces. Could it be otherwise? It was a failure in its conception; it must be a miscarriage on its birth. It was inevitable that a measure, by the mere *production already* of which ' *the debt to Ireland had been paid in full*;' yet of which on the one side it was said, ' *that a vote for it the country would regard as a vote of confidence in Cardinal Cullen and his priests* ;' whereas on the other side YOU *vehemently impeached* that very Roman prelacy of Ireland for its defeat: should not only disappoint, but be productive of discontent and acrimony; that it should stir up the muddy waters of so-called ' religious ' passions.

Though—the blessings of peace seemed once more to throw forth their enlivening beams over the Emerald Isle, and prosperity to smile upon its population. True to the proverb:

> Wer andern eine Grube gräbt
> Fällt selbst hinein,

the axe rebounded this time from the Upas Tree; it struck you, and under its vibrations the Gladstone Ministry, the brass idol of your unlimited greed for power, fell to pieces. Foiled in your pernicious schemes you retreated in your vapour bath of sanctimonious practices as to the best method of spending the closing years of your life. And though the Nation knew that in spite of, nay, over your pamphlets 'What is Ritualism?' and 'The Vatican Decrees in their bearing on Civil Allegiance,' you were hatching new plots against the Church, against Ireland, against the Empire; in favour of Ultramontanism; for the advancement of Fenianism— the patriots, not without some reason, thought Ireland and England at least for a while secure from the all-devouring English-Irish Moloch.

Indeed, their expectations were justified. Thanks to the renewal and prompt administration of the Peace Preservation Act, it could be stated of Ireland in 1875-76 'that at no time of its history did the Emerald Isle appear more tranquil, more free from serious crime, more prosperous and contented.'

However, though ostensibly retired from active politics, *you were still alive.* Nor were the demagogues thoroughly weeded out. *Could the peace thus last for long?*

Sir, you had grave reasons to apprehend that the desertion of your party would tell against you. Moreover, your rival Disraeli had successfully taken up the policy of an Elizabeth, a Cromwell, a Chatham, a Pitt. Convinced that *Great Britain limited to Great Britain* would soon roll down from her proud and above all commercially and industrially advantageous position of a first European Power, he endeavoured to extend her political sphere of influence in proportion to the rapid growth of her population. Being assured that in new foreign markets alone could be found relief for the flooded industries and over-crowded cities at home; and that the lustre of the Crown, the glory of the British name would shed economical and social blessing upon the Sister Isles—in the face of the envious nations abroad he unfurled the Imperial banner amidst the enthusiasm of the patriots of Great and the peoples of Greater Britain.

Your policy of dismemberment seemed thus doomed. And though yours was as yet only an eclipse in the light of his ascent; the longer your silence, the more problematic became your return to power. The shadows of a retired life, troubled by and breaking out in passionate fits of an abnormal conscience, began already to darken your 'fame.' It needed a new agitation.

One party was discontented with this Imperial policy. For them the 'civis Britannicus sum' doctrine had a hateful sound. It was the party of which you had once stated that *through them*:

'*The House of Commons would degenerate into an assembly of municipal and parochial minds*;' the party composed of '*little luminaries fitter for a municipal chamber than for the senate of the most extended empire in the world*;' the party of which '*you viewed with deep regret the undue predominance it gave to merely local ideas, a conduct which would threaten to leave the government of the greatest Empire in the world to be the prize of a scramble among a motley crowd of eager, contentious and egotistical mediocrities.*'

This party, this very party it was upon whose support you were thrown. Your last anchorage lay in Radicalism. There you had to fix your hold without delay, or else be swept from the scene for ever.

Alack, sir, only too willingly you espoused their narrow-minded contentions with all the clamour and pretension of a demagogue. Like a poisonous spider you stretched forth your insinuations as to the dreadful perils into which *Imperial* policy would plunge the country. You flung right and left the evil forebodings of an inevitable war with Russia. Your inflammatory harangues, they fell with the vehemence of volcanic eruptions upon the Nation until she was one glowing, boiling mass. And on it you rode to power.

But the commotion which bore you to the Government was wrought by deception. Your second Ministry was thus cursed to be *one continual* falsehood. Begotten in sin, it could not but lead to ruin: the wages of sin is death.

Ireland had to pay the penalty.

How well is all this illustrated by the Manifesto of my Lord Beaconsfield; how truly does it foreshadow the coming era of betrayal and faction; how fully does it characterise your position!

'The measures respecting the state of Ireland which

Her Majesty's Government so anxiously considered with your Excellency, and in which they were much aided by your advice and authority, are now about to be submitted for the Royal Assent, and it is at length in the power of the Ministers to advise the Queen to recur to the sense of her people. The acts of agitators which represented that England, instead of being the generous and sympathising friend, was indifferent to the dangers and sufferings of Ireland have been defeated by the measures at once liberal and prudent which Parliament has almost unanimously sanctioned.

'During the six years of the present Administration the improvement of Ireland and the content of our fellow-countrymen in that island have much occupied the care of the Ministry, and they may remember with satisfaction that in this period they have solved one of the most difficult problems connected with its government and people by establishing a system of public education open to all classes and creeds.

'Nevertheless, a danger, in its ultimate results scarcely *less disastrous than pestilence and famine*, and which now engages your Excellency's attention, distracts that country. A portion of its population is attempting to sever the Constitutional tie which unites it to Great Britain *in that bond which has favoured the power and prosperity of both.*

'It is to be hoped that all men of light and leading will resist this destructive doctrine. The strength of this nation depends on the unity of feeling which should pervade the United Kingdom and its widespread dependencies. The first duty of an English Minister should be to consolidate that co-operation which renders irresistible a community educated as our own in an equal love of liberty and law.

'*And yet there are some who challenge the expediency of the Imperial character of this realm. Having attempted and failed to enfeeble our Colonies by their policy of decom-*

position, they may perhaps now recognise in the disintegration of the United Kingdom a mode which will not only accomplish but precipitate their purpose.'

Indeed, sir, although by force of circumstances the Leader of Radicalism, with the exception of the enfranchising legislation, you had until then always looked with inward, with constitutional aversion upon the Radical programme of ' reforms.' But with an Ireland law-abiding and progressing the barrier would be removed which hitherto had stopped the flood of constitutional, political, economical, land, and sociological changes towards the triumph of a true Democracy. Whereas your mission was Anarchy; your ambition tyranny. *Upon Ireland, therefore, it was most expedient to hurl the new commotion.* For, writhing under the blight of further spasmodic, contradictory, conglomerate legislation, its convulsions could not fail seriously to affect the Nation and to absorb the very life interest of Radicalism. And, as if to further your pernicious expedient, once more the evil genius of Great Britain, nay, of Ireland, raised you your best allies amongst the Irish themselves. It sent another blight, a more terrible blight than had ever before befallen the Emerald Isle—it sent:

The Land League.

Behold, just as *you in England* could not succeed with an Ireland law-abiding, so *the Republican Brotherhood in Ireland* could not flourish with an Ireland contented. Upon a population constantly improving its moral and material position, thus becoming more and more reconciled to the existing *régime*, there was nothing for the demagogues to feed. Therefore their very existence was at stake, and to save it they were to make violent efforts. Under such conditions could it be otherwise than that your clamour should find a ready echo amongst Fenianism, and your scheme an ally amongst the lawless rabble, though as yet unconscious of the identity between your ambition and their aim?

Moreover, the teachings of the Butts and the Powers were rapidly paling. On the Irish horizon appeared the Parnell Comet. From the Irish soil sprung the Scorpion of the Land League, Michael Davitt. The doctrines of the Skirmishers, the Clan-na-Gael, the V.C., the American Nationalists began pest-like to seize the Home Rule party in the Emerald Isle. They soon infected the latter's aim. It was no longer an effort to place Ireland in the same relation to the British Empire that the State of New York bears to the Union. Their cry—their threat was henceforth for a national existence. But '*the peasantry in Ireland were in a dormant state.' The Separation movement hitherto had failed, according to the Father of the Land League, for two reasons:* First, 'because there had never been one in which the people were united;' second, 'because the movements had been wholly sentimental.' *It needed, therefore, something more luring; a something that did appeal to the prejudices of the people; a something that did excite the cupidity of man and inflame even his worst animal passions. Only by dint of work, great energy and incessant appeals to every feeling, every sentiment, every wrong, every superstition that would rouse the farmers, could the Land League be brought beyond the point to which these Butts had brought it in their drag-along movement. The Land Question furnished this all-powerful pretext.* It could not fail to invigorate a movement which in the words of Dillon '*would succeed and overthrow the first garrison of an alien and hostile government.'* Hence the Land League was organised, the characteristics of the formation of which and its principles have thus been explained by Michael Davitt:

'The principle upon which the Land League was founded is, as a matter of course, subject for dispute and difference of opinion, and *the programme* which was drawn up by the persons named (the American Nationalists) and *embodied in resolutions* of the Conference on October 21, 1879 (inasmuch as it did not comprise any demand for self-government), cannot be credited with containing the whole "principle" upon which the Land League was founded. *The organisers of the Conference had to consider the advisability of framing such a programme as would not " scare " any timid land reformer away from the projected movement, and it was further considered necessary to render it eminently constitutional for the double purpose of legal protection against the Castle and to enable members of Parliament to defend it within the House of Commons. What, then, was the principle upon which the Land League was founded ? I maintain that it was the complete destruction of Irish landlordism: first, as the system which was responsible for the poverty and periodical famines which have decimated Ireland; and, secondly, because landlordism was a British garrison,* which barred the way to national independence.'

Such were the avowed aims of the Land League: the severance of Ireland from England; the establishment of an Irish Republic.

Now by the force, the irresistible force of common personal interests and a common fatal mission, the champions of these pernicious teachings became henceforth your allies. It is true you were for a time still vacillating between coercion and felonious concession. But that your fresh career should end in a humiliating surrender to Fenianism, in a betrayal of your country, and become a curse on the Emerald Isle, was certain.

Already on the morn of your return to power you invoked the demons of discontent, greed, violence and hatred. *Though at the opening of this new 'Gladstonian' epoch there were once more endless, vitally important and urgent reforms to be dealt with in England, in Great Britain, in Ireland itself, the settlement of which was of scarcely a contentious character, and would have been beneficial to the Nation—* you introduced the infamously famous

Compensation for Disturbance Bill,

a 'legislative' proposal which could not fail to rouse the wildest passions.

But can you be blamed for its production?

It was the evil consequence of your first iniquitous measure, the first Land Act. You had legalised the doctrine of robbery, you had denounced the rights of ownership, you had punished loyal devotion to the interests of your country; it was in the nature of events that now at the first opportunity you should pronounce by this new proposal the final blessing. Moreover, it was the honest repayment of a bargain. The treacherous waves of Irish 'demagogy' had borne you to power. Lest they should swallow you now, or rise above your despotism, you had to conjure them. And what better victim could you fling into the all-devouring vortex of Irish faction than landlordism, the garrison of the Union?

However, the sacrifice was for once too much for the Nation; at the same time it was scornfully rejected by your allies, the Parnellites. And with the rapidity of lightning the bane fell upon your perverse action. You had to ask '*for additional powers necessary to secure protection for life and property and personal liberty of action.*' You had to bring in 'THE PROTECTION BILL' and 'THE ARMS BILL.'

Ah, sir, that these measures had been energetically carried out! But alack! *you* were in power. Not restoration, peace and prosperity; but commotion and annihilation were your life's support and life-mission. How significant is that doggerel which was at that time circulated amongst the Irish children for the formation of a children's Land League :—

> A is the army that covers the ground,
> B is the buckshot we're getting all round;
> C is the crowbar of cruellest fame,
> D is our Davitt, a right glorious name,
> E is the English who have robbed us of bread,
> F is the famine they've left us instead.
> *G is the Gladstone, whose life is a lie.*

You were doomed to prove it. You had betrayed the Irish vote by passing the Coercion Acts. You had now to betray confiding England. That you could deny it for the sake of the political security, of the morals of the generations to come! You knew that 'the appeals in this new departure in Irish national effort which were thus addressed to the peasant mind did not originate in the exalted patriotism of a Thomas Davis, nor excite the farmers to the practice of virtues of disinterested patriotism.' For, as Michael Davitt has afterwards candidly stated, '*the appeals were made to self-interest rather than to self-sacrifice.*'

You were likewise aware of Parnell's speech, delivered at Galway in 1880 :

> 'I wish to see the tenant farmers prosperous; *but large and important as is the class of tenant farmers,* constitut-

ing as they do, with their wives and families, the majority of the people of this country, *I would not have taken off my coat and gone to this work if I had not known that we were laying the foundations by this movement for the recovery of our legislative independence. Push on, then, towards this goal, extend your organisation, and let every tenant farmer, while he keeps a firm grip of his holding, recognise also the great truth that he is serving his country and the people at large, and helping to break down English misrule in Ireland.*'

You could not be ignorant of the vehement declarations against your country, such as Redmond's:

'*I say for one I have a great and another object in view in this land movement.* I am anxious that the peasants of Ireland should be *free and independent men. I am anxious above all that Ireland should be a free and an independent self-governing country.* And it is because I know by the history of the past that landlordism in Ireland has ever been the supporter of alien rule, and because *I know that to-day it is the only link which binds us in that hateful union to England—it is for that reason above all others that I, at any rate, am here to-day as a Land Leaguer.* Now, fellow-countrymen, I have said over and over again, and I repeat it here to-day, *that in this movement in Ireland we are only continuing and prolonging the same old struggle which has never ceased to be waged by Irishmen against foreign rule in this island. In the old days that movement had other names.* In the old days it was supported by other means, but to-day, on a constitutional platform, in working for the land, for the people, we, every man of us, are still continuing the struggle which our forefathers made on the hill-side and the valley when they laid down their lives for the independence of their country.'

You must have known Matthew Harris's:

> '*When we found reason and argument of no avail, we found it necessary to appeal to the passions of the people, to tell them how they were rack-rented by landlords, how they were exterminated by landlords, and tell them all the evils that could rouse up the passions and the "manhood" of the country.*'

You must have foreseen that any concession to, that any compromise with the Irish demagogues and Fenian Republicans would only lead to further extortions on their part. The goal of their ambitions—an Irish anarchy; the idol of their prayers—the destruction of England and the annihilation of the English; unless it was reached, unless it was fulfilled, they would march on 'through rapine and murder' till the last and great treason concession would be exacted from you. Parnell himself had triumphantly declared at Westport:

> 'And also there is really no reason why we should permit ourselves to be demoralised by the greatest concession of all. If you *obtain concessions* of right privileges, *such as the Irish Church Act and the Land Act*, you run no risk of demoralising yourselves. I have always noticed that the breaking down of barriers between different classes has increased their self-respect, and increased the spirit of nationality amongst our people. I am convinced that nothing would more effectually promote the cause of self-government for Ireland than the breaking down of those barriers between different classes. Nothing would be more effectual for that than

the obtaining of a good Land Bill—the planting of the people in the soil. *If we had the farmers of Ireland the owners of the soil to-morrow, we would not be long without getting an Irish Parliament. I do not intend to be demoralised myself by any concessions. While we are getting a concession we may show the Government a little consideration for the time being, and give them a* quid pro quo, *but after that the bargain ceases ; and when we have returned them a fitting return for what we have got, we are quits again, and are free to use such measures as may be necessary according to the times and according to the circumstances.* You have a great country to struggle for—a great country before you. It is worth a little exertion on your part; it is worth a little time. Do your best, and your country will thank you for it, and your children hereafter.'

As to the terrorism *the Land League—the National League*—would spread over the country you could not be doubtful. You had bargained with their rebel-organisers. Thus, if not already by intuition, or better, by the instinct of a kindred nature, *your intercourse* with them had made you acquainted with their ambitions and aims. Should you not know that for the Land League, for the National League to exist, the supreme life-duty of the demagogues was *relentless* and violent persecution of all their opponents? And could you ignore who were these opponents? Sir, alack, not for one moment did you—could you misunderstand that not merely the loyal, but all and every law-abiding, industrious and honest citizen would be proscribed by these Fenian mercenaries. To you it must have been known that whosoever dared refuse to join these conspirators and assassins was doomed and boycotted not only during his stay in this world, but would be persecuted into the grave. For, Parnell himself has admitted in the House of Commons that the practice of boycotting has been used not only against persons who 'robbed' their neighbours by taking their holdings from them, '*but it has been used against persons who refused to join the Land League, who refused to illuminate their houses, and who refused to subscribe to various popular movements. It has been used in a variety of other ways which merit the severity of the most stringent condemnation.*'

Yet, behold! in spite of all warning, you tried again your '*expiatory*' policy. Though, according to your emphatic declaration, the debt to Ireland was paid in full in 1873, though all 'Irish grievances' had been settled by you, though you knew that the fiendish attacks of Fenians and Moonlighters, of Skirmishers and Land Leaguers were waged against landlordism, because landlordism was the British garrison and a pillar of strength to the Union; you now brought forth

The Land Bill.

Ah, sir, **there is no greater or** more weird mystery than the lethargy of **the** Nation where **you** are concerned. The phenomenon of your **existence—the** havoc wrought by your career which, Phaeton-like, **has in its** fatal course set the Empire aflame—what are they when compared with the calamitous fact, that in the face of all, you **repeatedly** succeeded in beguiling a great, though unfortunately distracted Nation? For **you** have fed, you have lived, you have **grown upon the** self-immolated bodies of your own creation. You have advanced statements, and proclaimed with the fervour of an apostle prophecies which, **when** you had sufficiently be**numbed the** people, you then denounced, and which you swept away as soon **as** a new creed was more likely to further your despotism. You have reared your political power by piling legislative measures—your work—upon the ruins— **again** your work—of legislative measures, as **to** the adoption of which you at one time had declared with all the vehemence of an interested fanatic, **with** all the **cunning of** an ambitious false prophet, that they would bring the Nation into the haven of peace, and inaugurate an era of continual progress and prosperity ; that they would open the millennium. Therefore, could it be otherwise?— :

This Land Bill, it too, did not spring from a virgin soil. Nay, from the source whence it originated could grow no harvest plentiful, beneficial and advantageous, however auspicious the conditions of the season might have been. Being one of the many measures which upon your call and under the sanction of perjury and treason pullulated as it were from a field of mouldering legislative abortments and political victims—the sacrifices of ambition and despotism, the immolations of cowardice—it bore the sting of death, and would, epidemic-like, infect the Nation. A denial, as it were, of all former professions of faith, a refutation of pledges often given, an abandonment of all the principles which in times perhaps scarcely gone by—which but a few years before you had so boastfully displayed and so relentlessly advocated—this Land Bill could not but be corruptive and destructive in its effects.

Indeed, it contained all the elements of demoralisation, of public plunder, of treason-felony, of dissolution. Its provisions renounced the fundamental doctrines of government and the ethics upon which human society is erected. In fact, it overthrew the very same rules and precepts which you yourself had at one time and another pronounced as vitally essential to the moral health of the Body Politic, and which you praised as the panacea against material revolution.

'*Fixity of tenure wholly unsustained by the slightest attempt at reasoning.*' '*Perpetuity of tenure on the part of the occupier, a virtual expropriation of the landlord . . . the effect of which provision would be that the landlord became a pensioner and rent-charger upon what is now his own estate.*' '*Perpetuity of tenure, a phrase that you flatter yourself is a little going out of fashion. If "you" have contributed anything towards it "you" are not sorry*'—all these your denunciations of the most iniquitous '*propositions which, if adopted, would bring the most grievous evils upon the country, and against which you solemnly warn the Nation:*' they all, without exception, nay, rather more advanced, more developed, BECAME NOW EMBODIED IN THIS LAND BILL.

But more! Beyond the wildest expectation

of the Parliamentary rabble of Irish demagogues you even carried out the proposal to establish a department in the State's household which should reduce excessive rents, yet against which you had formerly inveighed most violently, of which you had exclaimed:

'I own I have not heard, I do not know, and I cannot conceive what is to be said for the prospective power to reduce excessive rents.' . . . Shall I really be told that it is for the interest of the Irish tenant bidding for a farm that the law should say to him ' *Cast aside all providence and forethought; go into the field and bid what you like; drive out of the field the prudent man who means to fulfil his engagement; bid right above him and induce the landlord to give you the farm, and the moment you have got it come forward, go to the public authority, show that the rent is excessive and that you cannot pay it and get released!* If I could conceive a plan, first of all for *throwing into* confusion *the whole agricultural arrangements of the country;* secondly, *for driving out of the field all solvent and honest men who might be bidders for farms, and might desire to carry on the honourable business of agriculture;* thirdly, *for carrying* WIDESPREAD DEMORALISATION THROUGHOUT THE WHOLE MASS OF THE

IRISH PEOPLE, *I must say it is this plan and this demand that we should embody in our Bill as a part of permanent legislation, a provision by which men shall be told that there shall be an authority always existing ready to release them from the contracts they have deliberately made.*'

Indeed, sir,

The Land Bill and Demoralisation!

Behold, in this you had for once prophesied true, only too true. 'The demoralisation *spread* throughout the whole of the Irish people;' nay, it infected even the English rabble; and, if not already unredeemably demoralised in matters politic, the effects of the Land Bill certainly poisoned *now* your political character for ever.

Ireland was henceforth whirled in a chaos of outrages, crime and murder, whilst England resounded with the impassionate accusations which you hurled against the Irish agitators. Your message of peace had once more become a challenge for the most cruel faction-warfare history has ever known. The compact of 'goodwill' and 'conciliation' between you and the Irish demagogues had festered the bitterest hatred. Indeed, the nations abroad beheld with bewilderment, they looked with scorn upon the vituperations and pranks of reciprocal revenge which you and your present Irish Parliamentary bosom friends were then performing.

It is true—it would be wicked to deny it—you exhibited a marvellous heroism in the part you were playing. You actually aimed, nay, you really struck a blow at the hydra heads which your policy had begotten. You sent the robber chiefs of the Irish 'Parliamentary' party to prison. And most worthy of remembrance *is that great event when—entertained at the Guildhall—you valiantly delivered the ever-memorable homily on the claims of law, public order, and loyalty to the throne and institutions of the country. When you triumphantly waved to and fro the telegram which had announced to you the recent arrest of your future aider and abettor, Charles Stewart Parnell. When the whole assembly, including men of the most opposite political opinions, rose to their feet and cheered loud and long. And when, after the applause had died away, you appealed to all the leaders of all the political parties to support the supremacy of the Imperial Parliament.*

Yet as to the events which thenceforth rapidly developed—your betrayal of Forster, the murder of Cavendish and Bourke, the release of Parnell, the Pact of Kilmainham, all these deeds at the shame and humiliation of which the friends of Great Britain in Europe may well have blushed for the beguiled Nation who seemed insensible to the mortal wounds which her 'Statesman' inflicted on her—had they not better be left hidden under the winding-sheet that, mercifully to you, covers the victims of your policy; had they not better remain buried in their premature grave?

Sir, how calamitously the demoralisation spread; how dreadfully the Nation was repaid for her trust in you; how venomous an end the unholy alliance between you, the 'British' Statesman and the emissaries of the American Fenians, the Clan-na-Gael, the Invincibles came to, is best shown by your and your English confederates' inflammatory harangues such as your onslaught on John Dillon:

'He comes here as the apostle of *a creed of force*, which is a creed of oppression, which is a *creed of the destruction of all liberty.*'

Such as your accusations of the Parnellites, the Land Leaguers, yet in whose services you have since enlisted as their 'bravo:'

(1.) '*For nearly the first time in the history of*

Christendom a body—a small body—of men have arisen who are not ashamed to preach in Ireland the doctrine of public plunder.'

(2.) 'Behind the commission of these—agrarian—outrages in Ireland there are influences at work higher than any that belong to those who commit them.'

(3.) '*These—Irish members—are not persons seeking amendment of the law. They are seeking to dismember the British Empire.*'

(4.) '*So that with fatal and painful precision the steps of crime dogged the steps of the Land League*, and it is not possible to get rid, by any ingenuity, of facts such as I have stated, by vague and general complaints, by imputations against parties, imputations against England, imputations against Governments. You must meet them and confute them if you can.'

(5.) 'The process called "boycotting" is, according to the hon. member (Parnell), a legitimate and proper process. What is meant by "boycotting?" *In the first place, it is combined intimidation. In the second place, it is combined intimidation made use of for the purpose of destroying the private liberty of choice by fear of ruin and starvation.* In the third place, that being what "boycotting" is in itself, we must look to this, that the creed of "boycotting," like any other creed, requires a sanction, *and the sanction of "boycotting," that which stands in the rear of "boycotting," and by which alone "boycotting" can in the long run be made thoroughly effective, is* THE MURDER WHICH IS NOT TO BE DENOUNCED.'

Such as your *peroration on the infamously famous, happily defunct Parliament at Stephen's Green*:

'It seems almost impossible that such events could have happened only ninety years ago, but *the present position of affairs in Ireland, with many of the Wolfe Tone type,* leads us to realise that if France was not too much occupied with thoughts of Germany there are adventurous spirits in her army who would be ready to repeat the enterprise of Hoche. *If Ireland had Home Rule given her to-morrow, she would use her power with the continued endeavour, consistent with all her recent utterances, of complete separation from England.*'

This *is the lesson of history as to the prospects of a successful experiment in Home Rule.*

'It is a great issue; it is a conflict for the very first and elementary principles upon which civil society is constituted. It is idle to talk of either law or order, or liberty, or religion, or civilisation if these gentlemen (the Irish Home Rulers) are to carry through the reckless and chaotic schemes that they have devised. Rapine is the first object; but rapine is not the only object. It is perfectly true that these gentlemen wish to march through rapine to the disintegration and dismemberment of the Empire, and, I am sorry to say, even to the placing of different parts of the Empire in direct hostility one with the other. That is the issue in which we are engaged. Our opponents are not the people of Ireland. We are endeavouring to relieve the people of Ireland from the weight of a tyrannical yoke.'

Corroborated by John Bright's:

'An Irish rebel party, the main portion of whose funds for agitation come directly from the avowed enemies of England and whose oath of allegiance is broken by association with its enemies.'

As well as by Sir William Harcourt's:

'The land agitation in their hands (the hands of the Irish Nationalists) is an agitation whose object is to destroy the Union of the Empire and to overthrow the established Government of the United Kingdom.'

Especially by Sir George Trevelyan's:

'If you want to get at the truth you must never forget *that there are two Irelands—the Ireland of men of all creeds, ranks, and callings, who, whatever else they may differ upon, unite in wishing to preserve law and order, and the right of every citizen to go about his business in peace and safety. . . . On the other hand stand the men who planned and executed the Dublin murders, the Galway murders, the boycotting and firing into houses, the mutilation of cattle, and intimidation of every sort and kind throughout the island.'* (1883.)

How demoralising the effects of the Land Bill were, is best illustrated by utterances such as John Dillon's:

'*Gladstone's reputation in politics is, I believe, a false reputation, and based upon a most extraordinary gift of skilful misrepresentation of fact.*' (1891.)

Such as Wm. Redmond's:

'*There is not a single man from Mr. Parnell down to myself who does not hate the Government of England with all the intensity and fervour of his heart.*' (1885.)

Such as J. O'Kelly's:

'*Should a war break out between England and any foreign Power within three months, every man capable of holding a gun will be found fighting for the enemy against Great Britain.*' (1885.)

But, above all, by the Parnellite manifesto of 1885 to the Irish voters:

'*In 1880 the Liberal Party promised peace, and it afterwards made unjust war; economy, and its Budget reached the highest point yet attained; justice to aspiring nationalities, and it mercilessly crushed the national movement of Egypt under Arabi Pasha, and murdered thousands of Arabs "rightly struggling to be free." To Ireland, more than to any other country, it bound itself by most solemn pledges, and these it most flagrantly violated. It denounced coercion, and it practised a system of coercion more brutal than that of any previous Administration, Liberal or Tory. Under this system juries were packed with a shamelessness unprecedented even in Liberal Administrations, and innocent men were hung or sent to the living death of penal servitude; 1,200 men were imprisoned without trial; ladies were convicted under an obsolete Act directed against the degraded of their sex; and for a period every* utterance of the popular Press and of the popular meeting was as completely suppressed as if Ireland were Poland, and the Administration of England a Russian autocracy.'

'We feel bound to advise our countrymen to place no confidence in the Liberal or Radical Party, and so far as in them lies to prevent the government of the Empire falling into the hands of a party so perfidious, treacherous, and incompetent. In no case ought an Irish Nationalist to give a vote, in our opinion, to a member of the Liberal or Radical Party, except in some few cases in which courageous fealty to the Irish cause in the last Parliament has given a guarantee that the candidate will not belong to the servile and cowardly and unprincipled herd that would break every pledge and violate every principle in obedience to the call of the Whip and the mandate of the caucus. We earnestly advise our countrymen to vote against the men who coerced Ireland, deluged Egypt with blood, menace religious liberty in the school, the freedom of speech in Parliament, and promise to the country generally a repetition of the crimes and follies of the last Liberal Administration.'

The Home Rule Phase.

But, sir, the gulf, the boiling gulf of hatred that surged between you and the Irish 'parliamentary' band, the mercenaries of American Fenianism, of the Invincibles and Dynamitards, of the men of the Skirmishing Fund—it should once more be overbridged; common ambitions, common aims, common tendencies and characteristics between you and them should spin the arches for a fresh alliance. *'The high sanction of "boycotting"—murder;' it should receive the high sanction of a 'British' Statesman, sir—of Mr. W. E. Gladstone, the Right Honourable.*

Indeed, rapid is the fall when once upon the downward course. Only too true it is that man pays off one debt to sin but to ensnare him deeper in another.

You had begun your Irish policy with an act which, considering the motives whence it had originated, your enemies rightly call sacrilegious. You had practised opportunism, and entangled yourself in a vicious labyrinth of concessions to threats and violence. Commencing with bribing those who could either frustrate or further the advancement of your ambitious, despotic aspirations, bribing them with the spoils of your raids on the ancient institutions of your country; upon the incorporated rights, properties and titles of its citizens; upon the Body Politic—it was inevitable that you should end with and under the attempt finally to destroy Great Britain. In pursuing the phantasmagoria of an '*Irish*' *settlement of* '*Irish*' '*grievances*' of which your bosom friend, Sir William Harcourt, so pertinently remarked: '*If the English, if Great Britain, if we* (*the Liberals*) *are to govern Ireland according to the ideas of Irish demagogues, I fear we shall find ourselves reduced to the consequences of not governing Ireland at all*'—you could not but pursue your own fate; though unhappily after each step of yours another chasm opened rolling forth poisonous fumes over the betrayed Empire. And, indeed, Nemesis at last alighted upon you.

You saw your power wane. You thought of a new union, nay, of a fresh conspiracy with the Irish 'parliamentary' band. Your demon whispered that your rivals, that the Conservatives might henceforth have the 'doubtful,' yet in your opinion all-important support at Westminster of the Parnells, the Redmonds, the

Tim Healyites and McCarthyites. And though on October 15, 1885, my Lord Rosebery had indignantly denounced what such an alliance would be, when he exclaimed:—

> '*The followers of Mr. Parnell do not give votes for nothing. I fear the result will be disastrous.* I don't profess to be a very imaginative person, but I confess that my imagination fails to lead me to what the practical result of that alliance may be. We know the friendly feeling of Mr. Parnell towards this country, and we may be certain that it is not England, or Scotland, or Wales that will benefit by this new and interesting alliance. *It is an alliance which has not merely struck a mortal stab at political principles, but it involves a danger to the Empire itself*:'

You committed the final deed, which, if not stayed in time, should annihilate the Nation, blotting out, as it were, with its curse the whole history of a stormy, yet just and glorious past of many centuries of British, of Imperial evolution. You yourself hastened to form—nay, to renew this unholy alliance with Parnell; and though my Lord Salisbury had at the outset of his interim Ministry sufficiently declared that he intended to restore order, to check terrorism, and to carry out the law in Ireland in the same manner in which it was administered in England, you made, as John Bright wrote you on July 4, 1886, '*a complete surrender' of the destinies of the Empire.* But were you not doomed to descend from this world's scene, a second Ephialtes and Attila in one, to descend to the memory of posterity as the 'great wrecker?' Was it not the consistency of your morbid conscience which, rather than that the Conservatives, the staple element in your Nation, should set the ever-corrupting example of such an abnormal alliance, prompted *you* to throw before the hungry pack of the Irish ' parliamentary' wolves the

Bill to amend the Provisions for the future Government of Ireland?

However, sir, is it necessary to enlarge upon the inevitable effects which the adoption of these provisions for the future government of Ireland would have had on the future existence of Ireland? Will it be advisable—Say, is it worth while to inquire into the possibility of a Legislature such as that lined out in clauses 9, 10 and 11 of your amending Bill, such' as could only be hatched in an abnormally fantastic, in an utopian—exuberant imagination? Verily, you may believe, if not already immortal for the implacable hatred you bear your country, posterity will remember you as the most scathing satire on the perverseness and absurdity and self-indulgence of a statesman; it will remember as the most comic illustration of human 'wisdom' these clauses of yours constituting a Legislative Body in Ireland, these clauses of yours so worthy of a Jules Verne's, of a Don Quixote's idiosyncrasies:

9.—(1.) The Irish Legislative Body shall consist of a first and second '*order.*'

(2.) *The two orders shall deliberate together, and shall vote together,* except that, if any question arises in relation to legislation or to the Standing Orders or Rules of Procedure or to any other matter in that behalf in this Act specified, and such question is to be determined by vote, *each order shall, if a majority of the members present of either 'order' demand a separate vote, give their votes in like manner as if they were separate Legislative Bodies;* and if the result of the voting of the two orders does not agree the question shall be resolved in the negative.

10.—(1.) The first '*order*' of the Irish Legislative Body shall consist of one hundred and three members, *of whom seventy-five shall be elective members and twenty-eight peerage members.*

(2.) Each elective member shall at the date of his election and during his period of membership be *bonâ fide* possessed of property which—

  (*a.*) if realty, or partly realty and partly personalty, yields two hundred pounds a year or upwards, free of all charges; or

  (*b.*) if personalty yields the same income, or is of the capital value of four thousand pounds or upwards, free of all charges.

(5.) The term of office of an elective member shall be *ten years.*

(6.) *In every fifth year thirty-seven or thirty-eight of the elective members, as the case requires, shall retire from office, and their places shall be filled by election; the members to retire shall be those who have been members for the longest time without re-election.*

(7.) The offices of the peerage members shall be filled as follows; that is to say—

(*a.*) Each of the Irish peers who on the appointed day is one of the twenty-eight Irish representative peers shall, on giving his written assent to the Lord Lieutenant, become a peerage member of the '*first order*' of the Irish Legislative Body; and if at any time within *thirty years* after the appointed day any such peer vacates his office by death or resignation, the vacancy shall be filled by the election to that office by the Irish peers of one of their number in manner heretofore in use respecting the election of Irish representative peers, subject to adaptation as provided by this Act, and if the vacancy is not so filled within the proper time it shall be filled by the election of an elective member.

(*b.*) If any of the twenty-eight peers aforesaid does not within *one month* after the appointed day give such assent to be a peerage member of the first order, the vacancy so created shall be filled up as if he had assented and vacated his office by resignation.

(8.) A peerage member shall be entitled to hold office during his life, or until the expiration of *thirty years* from the appointed day, whichever period is the shortest. At the expiration of such *thirty years the offices of all the peerage members shall be vacated as if they were dead*, and their places shall be filled by *elective members qualified and elected in manner provided by this Act with respect to elective members of the first order*, and such elective members may be distributed by the Irish Legislature among the electoral districts, so, however, that care shall be taken to give additional members to the most populous places.

(9.) The offices of members of the '*first order*' shall not be vacated by the dissolution of the Legislative Body.

(10.) The provisions in the Second Schedule to this Act relating to members of the '*first order*' of the Legislative Body shall be of the same force as if they were enacted in the body of this Act.

11.—(1.) Subject as in this section hereafter mentioned, the '*second order*' of the Legislative Body shall consist of two hundred and four members.

(2.) The members of the '*second order*' shall be chosen by the existing constituencies of Ireland, two by each constituency, with the exception of the city of Cork, which shall be divided into two divisions in manner set forth in the Third Schedule to this Act, and two members shall be chosen by each of such divisions.

(3.) *Any person who, on the appointed day, is a member representing an existing Irish constituency in the House of Commons shall, on giving his written assent to the Lord Lieutenant, become a member of the 'second order' of the Irish Legislative Body as if he had been elected by the constituency which he was representing in the House of Commons.* Each of the members for the city of Cork, on the said day, may elect for which of the divisions of that city he wishes to be deemed to have been elected.

(4.) If any member does not give such written assent within *one month* after the appointed day, his place shall be filled by election in the same manner and at the same time as if he had assented and vacated his office by death.

(5.) *If the same person is elected to '*both orders*,'* he shall, within *seven days* after the meeting of the Legislative Body, or if the Body is sitting at the time of the election, within *seven days* after the election, elect in which order

R

he will serve, and his membership of the other order shall be void and **be filled by a fresh** election.

Indeed, even the too confiding Nation roused herself against the absurdities of this your proposal. The people instinctively **felt** its incongruities. It recognised at once that such an **Assembly was doomed to be** abortive, resembling in its construction **an airy castle,** peopled by the phantastic **impossible creations of an** abnormal 'romancier.' And though **by its provisions you** virtually *disenfranchised* **Ireland, in so far as it would have henceforth no** representatives at **Westminster; though by the reserve** clauses **as to customs, as to the retention of the** Royal **Irish** Constabulary **under** the control of the British Imperial Executive, you made *for once* Great **Britain the** real **ruler over the** Emerald Isle; though you **brought forth at** the same time another 'conciliatory' **measure,**

The Land Purchase Bill,

by which **you gave to the Irish landlords** the **right to be bought out at from twenty to twenty-two** years' **purchase of** their judicial rents, with something extra **by way of** compensation for arrears;—though **by** this proposal, 'adopted under a serious conviction of honour and duty' you admitted the *particeps criminis* and proclaimed against all your former actions—in the face of all your former statements and declarations that England, that Great Britain had some obligations towards her garrison in Ireland: the Irish landlords:

Sir, once more your evil scheme rebounded upon you; once more you were crushed beneath it. Deserted by your noble friends, by such true patriots as his Grace the Duke of Argyll, his Grace the Duke of Westminster, by my Lord Hartington, by the Brights, the Chamberlains, the Goschens—you fell, a monument of shame. That you had sunk for ever! For then Ireland might at last have been safely steered into the haven of peace and prosperity. Aye, already, with a Balfour at her helm and a Salisbury in command, she was successfully braving the winds and breakers; she was entering the sheltered gulf. But—that it could have been otherwise!—her demon was still lurking for her: you were yet alive. And in spite of the beneficial and beneficent enactments and laws, encouraging the economical, social and moral development of the Emerald Isle, which were passed for the reviving country by a firm and for this very reason truly Irish-patriotic administration; in spite of the rays of intelligence, which the Parnell Commission, which the ever-memorable speech of Sir Henry James threw upon the infernal workings of the Irish demagogues and conspirators—a mist, a Gladstonian mist was again gathering over Great Britain and the Nation became more and more dangerously affected.

TWELFTH LETTER

THE IRISH GLADSTONIAN ERA AND THE HOME RULE BILL OF 1893

To the Right Hon. W. E. Gladstone, M.P.

Sir,—But, 'Tempora fugiunt et horæ et dies et menses.' The Empire is no longer held in disquieting suspense. The clouds of doubt which for seven years have hung threatening over England like sulphureous vapours that thicken round a volcano before its outbreak—they have burst at last. It has come to pass

> Mons parturibat, gemitus immanes ciens,
> Eratque in terris maxima expectatio;
> Quid ille pareret? At ille legem '*Proteam*' peperit;

namely:

The Bill for the ' better ' Government of Ireland.

Indeed, sir, before the Nation has arisen the grandiloquent Gladstonian mirage of a union of hearts; you may believe, the people stand dumbfounded which way to turn. As to your enemies, they confess themselves by its phantasmagoria utterly confounded. And behold! the Irish parliamentary rabble delights since its appearance in high pranks of Irish!—nay, of British, of English patriotism. The cockney Radicals are lying low in anticipation of the spoils that will fall into their claws in the inevitable fast-approaching confusion. The priests' anxiety—it has developed into conceit, and their Walshite and Jesuitic distempers seem completely muzzled. They read *Rome* Rule for *Home* Rule, and what that means is explained by you when you say:

'*No one can become Rome's convert without renouncing his moral and mental freedom and placing his civil loyalty at the mercy of another.*'

It is explained in the 'Freeman's Journal' of April 16, 1891:

'*No body of clergymen in Great Britain would venture to put forward such claims as some of the Catholic bishops have recently advanced in Ireland, nor would it be possible for any organisation of ministers of religion across the Channel to interfere in elections in the spirit and after the fashion marking recent contests in Ireland.*'

It is proclaimed by Dr. Walsh, the would-be Cardinal and Irish Pope:

'As priests, *and independent of all human*

organisations, they possess *an inalienable and indisputable* right to guide *their people* in this *momentous proceeding, as in every other proceeding where the interests of Catholicity as well as the interests of Irish nationality are involved.'*

But the Socialists, too, see behind the Home Rule Bill visions of their millennium. The Anarchists rejoice since its first reading that they, together with the Fenians and *Irish-American* dynamitards, have found in you the 'legitimate' expounder of their chaotic creed. And the anti-popish scruples—the terrors of a supremacy of the Romish antichrist, which have so often, like a horrible nightmare, harassed the Nonconformist and Dissenter-teetotal, the Welsh, the Sankey and Moody conscience—they, too, are lulled to sleep by that Bill for the 'better' Government of Ireland; for do not the Veto and Suspensory Bills nestle under its 'blessing' wings?

Ah, sir, well may you be proud of this your Home Rule Bill. Rightly has its announcement been hailed by all revolutionary elements. By it are scattered to the winds the warnings of even a Peel, your great teacher, as to the ruin of a policy of concession: 'I will do anything to conciliate any portion of the people of Ireland that is just towards them, just also towards others. But, alas! *we have had many warnings that conciliation and peace are not the necessary results of concession and of intended kindness.*'

By it are scattered into the empty air those ever-memorable, ever-true prophecies of that Sir Robert Peel: '*I can have no security for the protection of law, property, or individual liberty, so long as the slightest degree of influence is exercised over the ignorant population of Ireland by agitators and conspirators. . . . A separate Parliament in Ireland would amount to a disbanding of society; and, new relations having sprung up since the incorporation of the two countries, to retain Ireland after a dissolution of the Union within her proper orbit in the system of the Empire would require the might of that omniscient and omnipotent Power by which the harmony of the planetary system had been arranged and was sustained.*'

By it you have once more perjured yourself in your most solemn declarations. *By clause* 1 *of your* '*Protean*' *Bill you give to Ireland a Legislature. By clause* 9 *you grant her eighty representatives in the Imperial Parliament.* You make thus the Irish-American republicans more than ever the arbiter of England's destinies, inasmuch as in your 'plot for the "worse" government of Ireland' you have obediently carried out the instructions laid down by a William O'Brien (January 1892):

'We are all united in demanding that the Irish Parliament, while it acts within its own province, *shall be as free from Imperial meddling as the Parliaments of Australia and Canada—that is to say, practically speaking, as free as air.*'

And by your quondam friend—then victim—Charles Stewart Parnell:

'It is now known to all men that when our Parliament has been restored to us it shall have *power to make laws for Ireland, and that there shall be no English veto upon these laws except the constitutional veto of the Crown, exercised in the same way as in the Imperial Parliament.*'

Yet in 1886 you, the Right Honourable, had solemnly stated:

'*I never will be a party to any plan which gives to the Irish people a separate Parliament, and also gives them a voice in British affairs at home.*'

By it you consummate your pernicious, your unnatural policy of disintegration.

The new revolutionary proposal neither contains the clause of the old—the scheme of 1886:

19.—(1.) It shall not be lawful for the Irish Legislative Body to adopt or pass any vote, resolution, address, or Bill for the raising or appropriation for any purpose of any part of the public revenue of Ireland, or of any tax, duty, or impost, except in pursuance of a recommendation from Her Majesty signified through the Lord Lieutenant in the session in which such vote, resolution, address, or Bill is proposed.

Nor the clause:

12.—(1.) For the purpose of providing for the public service of Ireland the Irish Legislature may impose taxes *other than duties of customs or excise, which duties shall continue to be imposed and levied by and under the direction of the Imperial Parliament only.*

Nor the clause:

33.—(*a.*) The existing law relating to the Exchequer and the Consolidated Fund of the United Kingdom shall apply to the Irish Exchequer and Consolidated Fund, and an officer shall from time to time be appointed by the Lord Lieutenant to fill the office of the Comptroller General of the receipt and issue of Her Majesty's Exchequer and Auditor General of public accounts so far as respects Ireland; and

(*b.*) The accounts of the Irish Consolidated Fund shall be audited as appropriation accounts in manner provided by the Exchequer and Audit Departments Act, 1866, by or under the direction of the holder of such office.

But instead, it hands over to the Irish Parliamentary rabble all the powers of finance. Does not the 'improved' Bill enact that—

'*All matters relating to the taxes in Ireland and the collection and management thereof shall be regulated by " Irish " Act, and the same shall be collected and managed by the Irish Government, and form part of the public revenue of Ireland.'* (Bill, 1893, 10 (3))?

Does it not enact that :

Save as in this Act mentioned, all the public revenues of Ireland shall be paid into the Irish Exchequer and form a Consolidated Fund, and be appropriated to the public service of Ireland *by Irish Act ?*

Indeed, by the ' Bill for the "better" Government of Ireland,' you consummate your treason-felony against England, against the Empire.

Abandoned are the former encouraging safeguarding provisions, such as :—

18. If Her Majesty declares that a state of war exists and is pleased to signify such declaration to the Irish Legislative Body by speech or message, it shall be lawful for the Irish Legislature to appropriate a further sum out of the Consolidated Fund of Ireland in aid of the army or navy, or other measures which Her Majesty may take for the prosecution of the war and defence of the realm, and to provide and raise money for that purpose ; and all moneys so provided and raised, whether by loan, taxation, or otherwise, shall be paid into the Consolidated Fund of the United Kingdom ;

such as :—

3. *The Irish Legislature shall not make laws relating to :* (3) *The army, navy,* MILITIA, VOLUN-

TEERS, *or other military or* **naval** *forces, or the defence of the realm.*

Such **as** :—

22. (1.) The power of erecting **forts,** magazines, **arsenals,** dockyards, and other buildings for military or naval purposes;

(2.) The power of taking waste land, and, on making due compensation, any other land, for the purpose of erecting such forts, magazines, arsenals, dockyards, or other buildings **as** aforesaid, and for any other military or naval purpose, or the defence of the realm.

But instead, the '*improved*' ***Bill** abandons in Clause* 30 *the loyal Irish Constabulary to* **the tender** *mercies of* **the** *mercenaries* **of** *Irish-American dynamitards, of* **the Clan-na-Gael,** *of the Invincibles, of* **the** *men* **of** *the Skirmishing Fund.*[1] *It delivers* **the** *only guard, the only re-*

---

[1] 'The Skirmishing Fund,' of which the 'Irish World' gives under date August 28, 1880, the following information as to the motives for and aims of its formation:—

'Five years **ago** O'Donovan Rossa, through the columns of this paper, **made** known to the Irish people the idea of skirmishing. . . . He did not himself write the address that was published. **Rossa called for** $5,000. The first notion seemed to rise no higher than the rescue **of a** few Fenian prisoners then held in English gaols. He wanted badly to knock a feather out of England's cap. That sort of theatrical **work did not satisfy us.**

'**Nor did it** commend **itself to** some **others** either. Rossa then **said he was** willing to burn down some shipping in Liverpool. **Why not** burn down London and the principal cities of England? asked one of the two whom Rossa, in the beginning, associated with him in the movement. Rossa said he was in favour of anything. The question of loss of life was raised.

liable guarantee as to the true and prompt and honest fulfilment of Ireland's obligations and re-

Yes, said he, who has put forward the idea. Yes, it is war, and in all wars life must be lost; but in my opinion the loss of life under such circumstances would not be one-tenth that recorded in the least of the smallest battles between the South and the North. Some one suggested that plenty of thieves and burglars in London could be got to do this job. Here we interposed. Why should you ask others to do what you yourself deem wrong? After all, would it not be yourself that would be committing the sin? Gentlemen, if you cannot go into this thing with a good conscience you ought not to entertain the notion at all.

'Here now, two questions presented themselves: (1) Was the thing feasible? (2) If feasible, what would be the probable result?

'That the idea could be carried into execution, that London could be laid in ashes in twenty-four hours was to us self-evident. England could be invaded by a small and resolute band of men, say ten or a dozen, when a force of a thousand times this number, coming with ships and artillery, and banners flying, could not effect a landing. Spaniards in the days of the Invincible Armada, and Zulus to-day, could not do what English-speaking Irishmen can accomplish. Language, skin-colour, dress, general manners, are all in favour of the Irish. Then, tens of thousands of Irishmen, from long residence in the enemy's country, know England's cities well. Our Irish Skirmishers would be well disguised. They would enter London unknown and unnoticed. When the night for action came, the night that the wind was blowing strong—this little band would deploy, each man setting about his own allotted task, and no man, save the captain of the band alone, knowing what any other man was to do, and *at the same instant strike with lightning the enemy of their land and race*. . . . *In two hours from the word of command London would be in flames, shooting up to the heavens in fifty different places.* Whilst this would be going on, the men could be still at work. The blazing spectacle would attract all eyes, and leave the skirmishers to operate with impunity in the darkness.'

sponsibilities towards England—it delivers these faithful sentries of British integrity and Imperial supremacy to the tyranny and revenge of the Healyites and Redmondites.

And lest your pernicious plot might, in spite of these treacherous mines, so masterfully laid with all the 'mad' cunning of an abnormal hatred, ambition and despotism, at the last moment fail to explode; *you actually dare to ask the Nation for contributions in amounts of half millions to the Fenian—the Dynamitard—the Irish Republican Fund.* Is it that you are thus anxious to endow with British, with English money the Irish and Popish conspirators because of the probability *of an Anglo-American conflict? Is it that you wish to enable these traitor-demagogues not only hospitably to receive any enemy of Great Britain, but materially to aid him?*

Still, your 'Protean' Bill has some redeeming features.

It is true, in their refraction its hell-born origin and fiendish aims show forth only the more hideously.

It is true, in its principles as well as in its purports and provisions as to Irish autonomy, it is even devoid of originality, in that before the appearance of this your revolutionary 'legislative' abortment, there have been so-called 'Personal Unions' such as the old German, the holy Roman Empire (the laughing-stock of Europe) and Spain under Charles V.; such as Poland and Saxony under Augustus; such as England and Hanover under the Georges. And, indeed, the end of all these—it points a moral which may well once adorn the Home Rule tale.

It is true, that it endeavours to produce in the two British Isles the happily defunct, aye, happily decayed 'Deutsche Bundesstaat.'

It is true, that in the inevitable development of your pernicious project there will occur many a similarity of evil cause and ruinous effect to the rapidly developing, decomposing conflict in Scandinavia between the 'Riksdag' and 'Ridderhus' on the one side, and the 'Storthing'—the 'Lagthing' and the 'Odelsthing' on the other.

It is true, that in one point its destructive operation will be analogous to the events that come to pass in federate Canada. Without *provisions for the establishment of autonomous County Councils or sub-divisional Provincial Delegations by which a large minority, differing in religion and race from an antagonistic* majority, would successfully **be** protected against the latter's oppression, this your Home Rule Bill, it must—in Ireland: in the loyal, prosperous, industrious and noble Ulster—reproduce the evils which play such havoc amongst the Protestant population of British origin in the province of Quebec.

It is true—although surrendering all the **rights and powers of** government to the Irish Legislature—your Home Rule Bill yet contains **no clause** by which the garrisoning in Ireland **of a** British army of occupation is rendered unlawful. Indeed, it leaves **in the** Emerald Isle such regiments as are already quartered there. In this you judge *that their very presence will not only be a continual source of vexation to the Irish parliamentary rabble, but must sooner or later come into collision with the ultimate policy of the Walshes, the Egans, the Davitts, the Tim Healys, and* **the** *Redmonds.* It is true, therefore, that it contains all the combustibles for another civil war, worse than any ever before, a war which will only terminate after the annihilation of one of the combatants. Thus, so far your 'Protean' proposal is fiendish both in its origin and aim.

But, sir, notwithstanding, there are redeeming features. Sir, notwithstanding, there are two provisos which are really unique. They are inspired by the dictum:

> When two authorities are up,
> Neither supreme, how soon confusion
> May enter 'twixt the gap of both.

First, your Bill contains an all-important —nay, a patriotic!—preamble: 'Whereas it is "*expedient*" that without "*impairing*" or "*restricting*" the supreme authority of Parliament, an Irish Legislature should be created.' For, with such a preamble! can it matter much that there will be no longer a loyal Ulster and a loyal Constabulary to protect this supreme authority of the Imperial Parliament? With such a preamble! can it matter that in case of an Irish alliance with an American or French host against England; that in case of the triumph of Fenian terrorism and 'Irish parliamentary' anarchy the British troops might have to re-enforce this supreme authority perhaps at the point of the bayonet, yet no longer as the guardians of law and justice and in the interests, in fact, for the real benefit and protection of Ireland, but held up by the Irish traitor-demagogues as oppressors and hated aliens?

Secondly, there is a proviso in your Bill by

which the Lord Lieutenant is retained—the Lord Lieutenant! the representative of the Queen! His nominal continuation being thus guaranteed, *can it be of much consequence that he is virtually dependent on an 'Irish' Executive, which again is actually the instrument of the 'Irish' Legislature, swayed in turns by the rabble and the priests; sometimes coerced by both at one and the same time; fooling the Queen's representative, and tyrannising over the industrious, the real population of Ireland?*

No, sir, this your 'Protean' Bill, indeed, how wonderful it would work, if the patriots were less untractable!

Yet these patriots will not be persuaded otherwise. They contend that this your new Home Rule Scheme would, if passed, sever the bonds by which the British community is held together. *They maintain that it aims the death-blow at the rights and the security of property,* even where acquired by dint of industry, self-denial and thrift. They firmly believe that it *will poison the law and defame the administration of justice.* They say it establishes the *terrorism of the brutal force of numbers,* destroying for ever the equitable titles of minorities to state and defend their cause in a constitutional manner. They are convinced that by the adoption of its principles, *tolerance becomes a sham, and religion a pompous, theatrical farce of hypocrisy.* They apprehend, they vividly apprehend that the fulfilment of its promises to threats and murder, perjury and treason will tarnish the Nation's honour, and that *on the drooping banner of the Empire the peoples abroad, the foreign enemies of Great Britain shall read the infamous story how England, how a British Statesman could betray, and did betray their most sacred obligations towards thousands and thousands of loyal citizens and civil servants.* And though they have yet some hope that the time has still to come when the British Nation turns Judas against the British Nation, they look forward with terror to the mischief which *your attempt already at disintegration* must work. They believe that the baneful effect of this Home Rule Bill consists already therein that the very fact of you being suffered to produce such a traitorous, such a revolutionary, such a pernicious and unnatural proposal uncovers before the world a state of licence, of demoralisation, of decomposition, the knowledge of which will, pest-like, spread and further poison the people, the example of *which will corrode the very foundations upon which Great Britain has grown prosperous, glorious and peacefully great.* For they hold that the whole history of this infamously notorious Home Rule Bill, from the motive for its conception, from the hour of this conception, from the development, the growth of this conception to the hour of its birth and since, has been one continual perjury, and a depraved, or rather, a mad glorification of high treason, of felony and assassination.

THIRTEENTH LETTER

THE HOME RULE BILL'S EPITOME—
THE RIGHT HONOURABLE'S EPITAPH

To the Right Hon. W. E. Gladstone, M.P.

Sir,—Such is the 'legislative' measure by which you persuade yourself to solve the Irish problem. Truly, it crowns your phenomenal career. Under the bane of the solution you attempt, the Empire would crumble and revolution sweep its disjointed fragments into the chaos of destruction.

But dare it come to pass?

No, methinks I see in my mind the Nation rousing herself from a lethargic sleep. Methinks I see her rise, like a lion shaking his mane to the jackals and hyenas that were prowling closer and closer round their king, deeming him dead and an easy prey. Methinks I behold her as an eagle triumphantly soaring forth from an abyss, and kindling her undazzled eyes at the full mid-day beam of patriotism which at last has broken gloriously through the poisonous vapours of faction-strife. Methinks I watch her with 'bated breath now immerging into the boiling sea of political passion, but now emerging renewed in her existence like a phœnix, and more powerful, more noble than ever, more enlightened as to her mission towards the peoples, towards the nations that have gathered under her banner. And in the hour of this her triumph, methinks I see her even mourn over the great fall of one who might have been to her a blessing, both for his opportunities and his powers; but whose doom it was to become her curse. For your career and its catastrophe —though it has opened a hundred chasms that hungrily gape to swallow up the Nation, yet— should England not be grateful—it has uncovered, and it will reveal and expose in all their hideousness the parasites, the parliamentary rabble, the Home Rulers, these Walshites, these Healyites and Redmondites that are festering the Irish wound and keep her sorrows from healing. And perhaps the time will come that then the sons of Erin, too, shall awaken from their wicked dream and recognise at last the true freedom, the true liberty, the heavenly-born daughter—the freedom which an obedience to the law alone can confer. Perhaps the time will come when they will hurl their malediction at the phantom of national independence which has lured them for centuries into a desert of misery, massacre and crime; at the phantom of liberty which is but license, tyranny and anarchism.

Sir, but how will you then stand before the Irish people, and by what reasons will you justify your false gospel of the eternal rights of man and nationalities? The subtleties of your political metaphysics will be crushed by the gigantic weight of historical realities. In vain will you plead that, by overthrowing the barriers which convention and its effect, society, have raised and the rules they have laid down for the formation and the protection of States without which there can be no advancement in civilisation, you have restored to the Irish the original birthrights of a state of nature. From evil can come no good, and you knew, from the rapidity with which the revolt of America begot the revolution in France, how quickly grows and swells the hurricane of rebellion that must break up all the foundations upon which not only Great Britain but all the truly great Empires are towering. But will you really end your life by that tragic, by that infernal act; by casting, in the name of liberty, Ireland into the dungeon of despotism, and, through the example you set, all other nations into the conflagration of racial, of tribal ambitions and wars?

That you would have remembered the eternal law of nature by which the smaller atoms are by the larger particles with which they come in contact attracted, assimilated and converted into one solid, one united mass! Ireland's march towards progress would never have been impeded, and the Emerald Isle, Great Britain were not threatened now by a British statesman with destruction. For the burning and inflaming lava of your legislative schemes must destroy all life, if not stemmed in time.

But is not destruction reconstruction? Are not all endings said to be new beginnings?

Indeed, behold on the firmament yawns infinite night: the huge grave of planets that have devoured themselves in their heat unspeakable. But ere long, where there was darkness, there new stars blaze up. And they pass on and enlighten and enliven. Then they flicker again into dimness.

These phenomena of stellar-collisions are they not phenomena of such evolution? For in that crucible of change, full of flame and fury of liquefaction, of elements bubbling and roaring in the process of their decomposition, new destinies are shaped.

Aye, as it is with stars, even so it is with nations. Whilst those roll in their orbs, these move in their spheres towards their common end—for a common purpose. They are all ephemeral: the days of men, the lives of nations, the ages of planets. None will escape destruction, so that new life may spring from their ruins.

But, sir, *these new destinies, these new creations are worked out upon eternal laws. No star shall fall from its ellipse until its hour has ripened; nor shall any nation die before it has conceived the germs for the birth of a new people.* Therefore, stay! Beware, you waste your last powers. Hold back or you will damn even the final stage in your life when you should strew that seed the fruits of which would shine for you in heaven, and which might move the angels to blot out with their tears of mercy the record of your former misdeeds. Sir, in vain you attempt, in vain you plot to hasten the combustion of the Empire. *The mission of the British Nation is not yet fulfilled. She shall not perish before that fulfilment.*

You have mistaken the temper of the people. You also mistake the purpose of your century. It is true it is an age of revolution. But it is not during *its* passage that the stormy season will open when mighty Empires such as Great Britain shall be broken up into atoms of nationalities. On the contrary, it is an era of concentration, of centralisation; and he it is that will perish who thrusts his arm between the wheels of that evolution.

In this you are right: there are States-unions; there are States-federations which are tottering towards their decay. *Behold Scandinavia, behold Austria, behold Turkey!* These are fast approaching their dissolution, for they have been raised *upon a patchwork of compromises and treaties; their policy is opportunism.* They vegetate within the vicious circle of self-governing, provincial, tribal, and small national legislatures, and of Imperial diets and royal delegations. They are worn out by the collisions between these their various governing bodies, each moved by its own principles and driven by its particular aims; in most cases the one directly opposed to the other. These countries, not unlike the idol made up of fragments of clay, iron, brass, silver and gold, that fell to pieces before the dawn of a better creed; they will be swept away ere long by that irresistible movement. Their tottering composites will soon be thrown into the furnace of re-creation, there to be melted down and then to be driven into new forms more in harmony with the age, so that the hundred features of their hundred nationalities will be effaced, and the new nation bear the impress of one uniform character. And there will be models. There shall be Great Britain. There will be Germany, for '*Deutschland, Deutschland* über Alles' is the dream and the hope of the coming German generations.

Indeed, such is the course of civilisation; that there shall be an international union of large States with an international board of arbitration. Can there be any longer room for every tribal claim for a national independence?

No, sir, the larger the Empires, the more numerous their populations, the more often will points of dispute between the various countries be treated from a lofty, from a calm and unbiassed, from an international standpoint, the less frequent will such contentious questions crop up, *because the petty jealousies of small rulers, the distempers of ministers, the fancies and revenges of mistresses, the tribal pedantries and ambitions of tiny nationalities will no longer be an element of disturbance, but henceforth be sunk in the great considerations of commerce and industry, and education and science—of civilisation;* because also the different Governments dare no longer plunge their millions and millions that make up the various great nations they represent, into wars which must end in the ruin of both the belligerents. *Nor will these peoples themselves easily be moved to rush into such wars; they will pause before they risk, unless it be for tremendous issues, a struggle that must be a struggle of extermination of the one combatant, that must be a war of destruction to the other combatant.*

Therefore, abandon—it is the last moment—fling from you your policy of disintegration. Great Britain, the British Empire shall yet live; she must yet rule over the sister isle, over her peoples abroad. In vain you stem yourself against the tide of that great evolution. Not yet is Great Britain's imperial mission fulfilled. Nay, it has only just begun. And you cannot destroy her and cast the Irish, cast the African, cast the Hindoo upon the ocean of dismemberment—a wreckage of worse than helpless orphans.

No, your attempts must end in **your** self-destruction. Behold the bloody battlefields of Missolonghi, of Solferino, of Königgrätz, and Sedan—they proclaim that there shall be but great nations in which the surrounding **tribes and** small nationalities are swallowed up **in the interests** of progress, of society, of **civilisation.**

Sir, such has been the life-principle **in** the growth of nations before **the** Romans; **it** has been the motive in the formation **of States from** the dawn of history.

Indeed, vainly you **would compare the Roman** Empire—the *end* of the Roman Empire—with the prospective end of Great and Greater Britain. Sir, it has been admitted that **the life of** states is like the **life of** man: it has a beginning and a termination, **and to this law the** British Empire is subjected. But **again and again** be it said, and the Nation will soon **proclaim** it when thundering forth **your condemnation, the con**flagration of Great Britain **is yet** chained up in a far-off future.' If Rome, **the** Imperial Rome, fell within a few centuries **of its** birth, **it** was because Rome did **not** spread the blessings of civilisation amongst her nationalities. Rapine and plunder was her aim, and instead of flourishing cities and fertile plains, she left deserts **in**

T

her track. But Great Britain's mission is an *apostolic* mission. And centuries after, when of you and your **Irish** conspirators there will not be even one grain of mouldering dust, she will **still** fulfil this her glorious mission, nobly, unswervingly, beneficently, and beneficially; **she will still rule** the **waves**—**the** Empress of the **oceans;** and **under the** protecting shadows of her Imperial banner will still gather the grateful **peoples that now live** prosperous and happy **within the pale of Great and** Greater Britain. And Ireland will think **with horror** of her former wicked **dreams; she will** think with horror of her traitor-demagogues. She **will have** sought **new** modes of **action.** With true men to guide **her she will have** found **and** bravely pursue **these new paths. And on her, too,** will be poured the blessings **of** contentment and peace.

Sir, as to yourself—such will be your end: self-destruction. And thus it shall come to pass that the long discord which has been jarring throughout your political career, terminates in one weird, hitherto unheard-of dissonance, the vibrations of which may well spread terror among the Nation and cause consternation in the peoples abroad.

Verily, you may believe, already for the sake of your age which overshadows my years by three score and more, I would have wished to speak of you in terms of praise and enthusiastic gratitude; for the sake of your undaunted perseverance, which, though employed in a fatal cause, yet brilliantly shows *the moral purity of your private life*, I would have desired to be able to hold you up to the Nation—to posterity, a genius of statecraft and a symbol of patriotism. But as I turned over the leaves of your political record, I found but dark spectres such as may herd in the sterile despair of an Arctic winter night. No lights to guide the coming generations, no revelations to elevate their political morals beamed upon me; no sparkling fountains that might refresh the patriotism of the Nation bubbled forth, encouraging me as I mournfully passed along on my onward march through the gloomy labyrinth of your political life. There—whilst I tremblingly stood, whilst I fain was turning to flee from so uncanny a spectacle, I was, as it were on a sudden, confronted with the monster of that cave. Upon me stared the phantasm begotten of a wizard—your Home Rule Scheme. And, sir, although not born in nor reared by this country, I now felt my blood tumultuously rising. For tremendous are the issues that, like the sword of Damocles, hang on the thin thread of your advanced life not over England, not over Great Britain alone, but over Europe, threatening her nations with dissolution and destruction! Thus I venture it, thus I appeal to you, abandon your pernicious scheme; thus I call upon a noble Nation to rouse herself, and if *you* will not give way, to crush you and your satellites beneath *her*.

Indeed, willingly would I have employed other methods. But the subject of your career can only be treated in a language befitting it. If that language has been impassionate, you have provoked it. It is the language of the heart; it is the echo of the curse of your deeds.

Verily, you cannot blame the patriots that they are doubtful whether of you may be said:

'REQUIESCAT IN PACE.'

INDEX

ACT, Crimes, 198
— Deasy's, 180
— Employers' Liability, 113
— Encumbered Estates, 179
— Habeas Corpus, 53, 180, 190
— — — Suspension, 194
— Irish University, 102
— Peace Preservation, 204
— of Settlement, 53
— — Uniformity, 141
— — Union, 160
— Treason Felony, 190
Afghanistan, xi., 101, 105
Alexandria, burning of, 103
America, 40, 44, 45, 99, 265
Anarchism, 78, 83
Apology of Mr. Gladstone to Austria, 97
Arabi Pacha, 231
Archbishop of Dublin, murder of, 137
Argyll, Duke of, 241
Aristotle, his ideal State, 39
Armenia, xi.
Arms Bill, the, 214
Athenree, battle of, 133
Attainder, ix.
Australia, 16
— abandonment of, ix.
— Colonies Bill, 12
— supports Britain, 46
Austria, 75, 97, 268
Aylesbury Election, 85
Ayoob Khan, 105

BALFOUR, Mr., 241
Balkan Peninsula, 97
Beach, Sir M. H., 16
Beaconsfield, Earl of, 99, 189, 191, 205, 207
Ben Jonson, 33
Bismarck, 100, 111, 112
Black Sea, xi., 99
Boulanger, General, 43
Boycotting, 154, 219, 227
Brehon Law, 133
Brennus and his Gauls, 67
Bribery in House of Commons, 84
Bright, John, on Home Rule, 229, 235
— — leaves Mr. Gladstone, 241
Bruce, Edward, in Ireland, 132
Brutus, 44
Bulgarian horrors, 18, 101
Bulwer Lytton, Sir Edward, on Gladstone, 102
Butt, Mr. Isaac, 210

CABINET, the British, 39
Cabul, 105
Canada and Mr. Gladstone, 99
Canal, Suez, x., 46
Candahar, 105
Cardinal Cullen, 203
— Manning, 29
— Newman, 29
Catholic Emancipation, 7
Catiline, 33, 154

CAU

Causes of the Irish Famine, 169
Chamberlain, Mr., leaves Mr. Gladstone, 241
Charlemont, Lord, 154
Charles I., fate of, 51
— — Parliament of, 85
Charmer, the Grand Old, xiii.
Charta, Magna, 49, 50, 75
Chatham, Earl of, 101, 205
Cicero, quoted, 39, 41, 57, 72
Civil war, 12
— — in America, 101
Clan-na-Gael, 182, 199, 210, 252
'Classes' against 'Masses,' 60, 61
Clerkenwell outrage, 190
Cochin China, x.
Collier, Sir Robert, 94
Colonisation of Ulster, 143, 144
Commons, House of, 39, 82, 84, 85
— — — its Constitution, 86
Commutation of Tithes in Ireland, 177
Compensation for Disturbance Bill, 213
Congress of United States, 40
Conservatives, the Legislative Measures of the, 113
Constantinople, ix.
Constitution, British, 37–54
— — its stability, viii.
— — — characteristics, 41
Corpus Act, Habeas, 53
— Habeas, Suspension Act, 194
Council, Common, 49
— County, 47
— Grand, 49
— Privy, 75, 94
Count of Egmont, 45
— Horn, 45
Courts, Hundred, 47
Crimean Campaign, 18, 101
Cromwell, 83, 138, 144, 205
Crown, the, 39
Cullen, Cardinal, 203

ELE

Cyprus, 99
Czar Nicholas, 16
Czechs, 7

Dante, quoted, 96
Dardanelles, xi.
Davis, Thomas, 215
Democracy described, 45
— a tyranny, 5
— Gladstone, a champion of, 13
Denmark, 101
Derby, Lord, on Irish Church Question, 190
Dermod, King of Leinster, 129
Despotism, 41
Deutsche Bundesstaat, the, 255
Dillon, John, 211, 226, 230
Disestablishment of Church of England, 30
— of Church of Ireland, 13, 188
— of Church of Scotland, 30
— of Church of Wales, 30
Disraeli (see Beaconsfield)
Doellinger and Gladstone, 12
Dublin, murder of Archbishop of, 137
Dutch, the, 44

Earl of Beaconsfield, 99, 189, 191, 205
— of Derby, 190
— of Granville, 32
— of Strafford, 4
— of Tyrone, revolts of, 143
Edward I. in Ireland, 132
Edward III. in Ireland, 132
Edward V. in Ireland, 134
Edward VI. in Ireland, 139
Edward Bruce in Ireland, 132
Egmont, Counts of, 45
Egypt, 101, 104
— and Gladstone, 17, 231
— and Gordon, 16
— the gate to India, 16
— surrender of, ix., x.
Elections, Aylesbury, 85
— Middlesex, 85

ELI

Elizabeth, Queen, 51, 84, **205**
Emancipation, Catholic, 166
Emmett, Robert, rebellion of, 167
Estates, the Three, **42**

FAMINE, **the Irish, its causes,** 169
Fenianism, 178
— its characteristics, 182
Fitz-Stephen, **130**
Forster, Mr., **and Ireland, 174,** 225
France, ix., x., 43, 45, **112**
— and Ireland, 155, 162, **199**
— Chamber of, 40
— Senate of, 40
Franchise Bill, the County, 87
Franco-German War, 99, 199
'Freeman's Journal' on the Priest in Politics, 246
French Revolution, **the, 43, 57,** 181, 265
Frere, Sir Bartle, 96

GALWAY, Mr. **Parnell at, 215**
Gavelkind, 128
General Boulanger, **43**
— Gordon, 15
George I., 51
George III., 163
Germany, 255, 269
Gladstone, the Right Hon. W. E., his various aspects, vii.
— as a Private Citizen, **vii., xiv.,** 273
— a Tory, 4
— a Peelite, 11
— a Puseyite, 11
— a coquet, 16, 72
— an ecclesiastical broker, **29**
— and Mirabeau, 17
— a purist, 14, 23, 27
— plots with Fenians, 24, 204, 247
— a Scripture reader, 28
— the Opportunist arch-Jesuit, 30

GLA

Gladstone, the Right Hon. W. E., the Woodcutter, 34, 90
— a champion of Democracy, 12, 53
— an old Parliamentary hand, 84
— a hunter of phantoms, 106
— a disintegrator of Empire, 107, 263
— a Wrecker, 112, 197, 200, 236
— a follower of Lord Charlemont, 154
— a Betrayer of Pledges, 165
— a Breaker of Contracts, 197
— an Incendiary, 189
— a False Prophet, 221
— the arch-Opportunist, 154, 190, 195, 198, 233
— the Grand Old Charmer, xiii.
— Chief of the Lawless in Europe, 7
— compared with Absalom, 18
— — Catiline, 33, 95
— — Ephialtes and Attila, 236
— — Kleon, 94
— — Herostratus, &c., 95
— — Don Quixote, 98, 237
— — Jules Verne, 237
— and Doellinger, 12
— and General Gordon, 15, 16, 96, 103
— and Michael Davitt, 18
— and Jesse Collings, 21
— and Sir Robert Peel, 14, 107, 247
— and Mr. Forster, 225
— and Parnell, 22, 24, 26, 27, 225
— and Archbishop Walsh, 23
— and Lord Salisbury, 87
— and Lord Hartington, **31**
— and Lord Granville, 32
— and Sir Robert Collier, **94**
— and Sir Bartle Frere, 96
— and Sir Gerald Portal, 96
— and Count Karolyi, 97
— and John Dillon, 226
— and John Morley, 201

Gladstone, the Right Hon. W. E.,
and Homer, 31
— and Virgil, 82
— and Egypt, 17, 99, 104
— and the Ionian Islands, 98
— and Belgium, 99
— and Batoum, 108
— and Kars, 108
— and Cyprus, 99
— and Penjdeh, 108
— and Merv, 108
— and Ireland, 123 and following
— and the Phœnix Park Murderers, 191, 226
— endangers the Empire, xiv., 106, 204
— deserts Board of Trade, 13
— abandons Chancellorship of Exchequer, 15
— betrays the South African Colonies, 21
— abdicates leadership of the Liberal party, 31
— attacks House of Lords and aims at its destruction, 59, 73, 94
— creates a multitude of peers, 71
— apologises to Austria, 97
— defends the Boers, 98
— pleads for Russia, 98
— pays the Alabama claims, 99
— defends Crimean war, 101
— denounces Crimean war, 102
— establishes the Irish anarchy, 168, 172
— denounces Home Rule, 200, 229
— attacks the Land League, 227
— impeaches the Irish Catholic prelacy, 203
— releases Fenians, 178, 194, 198
— notorious for perversion of facts, 176
— guilty of high treason, 168, 199
— charged with moral assassination, 22

Gladstone, the Right Hon. W. E., charged with cowardice, 28, 30
— — Jesuitism and Popery, 28
— — treason, 21, 43, 251
— a diplomatist, 95
— Lord Beaconsfield on, 189
— contrasted with Pitt, 165
— author of 'The State in its Relation to the Church,' 13
— — 'Letters from Naples,' 17, 101
— — 'The Church of England: is it Worth Preserving?' 29
— — 'The Vatican Decrees in their Bearing on Civil Allegiance,' 29, 153, 194, 202, 204
— — 'Vaticanism,' 29, 153, 194, 202
— — 'What is Ritualism?' 204
— — 'Bulgarian Horrors,' 101
— at the Mansion House, 94
— at the Guildhall, 225
— at Manchester, 102
— at Aberdeen, 200
— and the British Constitution, 37, 48, 52
— and the Anarchists, 83, 168
— and bribery, 84, 233
— and Household Suffrage, 88
— and Manhood Suffrage, 88, 90
— and political jobbery, 94
— and the Fenians in Canada, 99
— and the Franchise, 121
— and the Church, 121
— and the Irish Church, 187, 190
— and the Government of London, 94
— and Education, 120
— and Social Legislation, 120
— and Fenianism, 178, 194, 198, 213
— and Separation, 202
— and the Radicals, 86, 88
— and the 'Maynooth Bill,' 11, 14
— and the 'Australian Colonies Bill,' 11

GLA

Gladstone, the Right Hon. W. E., and the 'Ecclesiastical Titles Bill,' 11
— and the 'Irish Disestablishment Bill,' 29, 187
— and the 'Irish University Bill,' 29, 202
— and the 'Public Worship Regulation Bill,' 29
— and the 'Land Purchase Bill,' 240
— and the 'Endowed Schools Act Amendment Bill,' 29
— and the 'County Franchise Bill,' 87
— and the 'People's Bill,' 77, 90
— and the 'Foreign Enlistment Bill,' 98
— and the first 'Irish Land Bill,' 178, 195, 213
— and the 'Land Bill,' 220
— and the 'Irish Glebe Lands Bill,' 192
— and the 'Irish University Bill,' 203
— and the 'Encumbered Estates Act,' 179
— and 'The Crimes Act,' 198
— and the Midlothian Campaign, 94
— his foreign policy, 105 and following
— his ecclesiastical policy, 121
— like a poisonous spider, 207
— and the 'Compensation for Disturbance Bill,' 213
— and the 'Protection Bill,' 214
— and the 'Arms Bill,' 214
— like Phaeton, 220
— his act of moral *felo de se*, 222
— imprisons Mr. Parnell, 225
— and the Land League, 226
— and 'boycotting,' 227
— and the Home Rule Bill of 1886, 236
— and the Home Rule Bill of 1893, 245

IMP

Gladstone, the Right Hon. W. E., and the Dissenters, 247
— and the Veto Bill, 247
— and the Suspensory Bill, 247
— his epitaph, 263
Gordon, General, 15
Goschen, Mr., leaves Mr. Gladstone, 241
Granville, Earl, 32
Grey, Lord, on Gladstone, 180
Guizot, 43

Habeas Corpus Act, 53, 180, 190
Hadrian IV., Pope, 129
Hallam, quoted, 76
Harcourt, Sir William, on Home Rule, 229, 234
Harris, Matthew, quoted, 217
Hartington, Lord, 31
Hawarden, 28, 30
Healyites, 7, 26, 28, 158, 235, 254
Henry II., 129
Henry III., 132
Henry VII., 51, 137
Henry VIII., 13, 51, 84, 137
Herostratus, 95
Herrenhaus of Prussia, the, 75
Hoche, General, 162, 228
Home Rule, 48, 185, 200, 227, 233
— — in Scandinavia, 255
— — in Canada, 255
— — Bill's Epitome, the, 263
— — Bill of 1886, 236
— — — of 1893, 245
Homer, quoted, 93
Hope, a friend of Gladstone, 29
Horace, quoted, 15
Horn, Count of, 45
House of Commons, 39
— of Lords, 39, 58
Hundred Courts, 47

Impeachment of Ministers, ix.

INDEX

IMP

Impeachment of Gladstone, 168
India, x., 100
— and Egypt, 16
International Law, x.
Ireland, 123
— betrayal of, ix.
— in the eighth century, 127
— polygamy in, 128
— tanistry in, 128
— gavelkind in, 128
— under the Plantagenets, 126
— conquest of, 127, 130
— lawlessness of, 131
— bloodshed in, 127
— under John, 131, **132**
— **under** Edward I., III., and V., **132, 134**
— under Richard II. and III., 133, 134
— **under** the Tudors, 136
— **under** Elizabeth, 140
— **under James** II., 144
— **under** Cromwell, 144
— **under an** Irish Parliament, **155, 161, 228**
— under Pitt, 159, 163
— Henry VIII.'s policy in, 138, 154
— a Papal lever for England's overthrow, 142
— a *place d'armes* for England's foes, 143, 254
— a traitor during the American Rebellion, 155
— a traitor during the Indian Mutiny, 182
— in league with France, 155, 162
— its ultimate aim—Separation, 157, 208, 211
— a Republic, 198, 212
— colonisation of Ulster, 143
— massacre of 1641, 145
— oppressed, 151
— her peasantry, 151, 216
— and the Penal Laws, 152
— and boycotting, 154, 219

JOH

Ireland and moonlighting, 154, 197
— and secret societies, 154, 167, 170, 174
— and the Presbyterians, 155, 164
— and Catholic emancipation, 166
— and O'Connell, 168, 176
— and the Famine, 169, 173
— and Mr. Forster, 174, **225**
— and Drummond, 176
— and Smith O'Brien, 180
— and Sadleir and Keogh, 181
— and the Navigation Laws, 152, 176
— and the Black Year, 171, 176
— and Commutation of Tithes, 177
— and Fenianism, 178, 182
— and the Invincibles, 182, 226
— and the Irish Church, 141, **187**
— and the first Irish Land Bill, 195
— and the Crimes Act, 198
— and the Irish University Bill, 202
— and the Encumbered Estates Act, 179
— and the commencement of opportunism, 154
— **and the** Land League, 210, 212
— **and landlordism,** 212, 216
— and the Home Rule Bill of 1886, 236
— — — — of 1893, 245
Irish Gladstonian era, the, 187
'Irishman,' the, 199

JAMES II., 51
— — Parliaments of, 85
James, Sir Henry, on Parnell Commission, 241
Jesse Collings, 21
Jesuitism, 12, 29, 30
John, King, and Ireland, 132

John, Prince, in Ireland, 131
John de Witt, 45
Jonson, Ben, 33

KASSALA, 103
Keogh and Sadleir, 181
Khartoum, 15, 103
Kilkenny Statute, 133
Killala, French land at, 162
Kilmainham Treaty, 23, 226
Königgrätz, 271

LABOUCHERE, xiii.
Lacy, 129
Lamartine, 43
Land Bill, First Irish, 178, 195
Land League, the, 210, 212, 218, 226
— the Children's, 215
— the National, 218
'Land Purchase Bill,' the, 240
Laocoon, 82
Law, International, x.
— Brehon, 133
Lecky, Mr., quoted, 177
Leinster, Dermod, King of, 129
— Rebellion in, 139
Liberals, their legislative measures, 113
Livy, quoted, 67
London, Corporation of City of, 45
Londonderry, Siege of, 144
Lord Charlemont, 154
— Rockingham, 156
Lords, House of, 39, 58
— — Constitution of, 62, 74, 76
— — a Court of Review, 63
— — a Constitutional Pillar, 39
— — a Constitutional Pilot, 65
— — a breakwater, 67
— — a reward, 68
— — a barrier, 70
— — its usefulness, 65
— — its composition, 66
— — its independence, 66, 74
— — attacked by Gladstone, 59

Lords, House of, destruction of, aimed at by Gladstone, 73
Louis Blanc, 43
Louis Buonaparte, 43
Louis XI., 43
Louis XIV., 43, 144
Lytton, Sir Edward Bulwer, 102

MCCARTHY, Justin, 28
McCarthyites, 235
'Macbeth,' quoted, 82
MacMahon, Marshal, 43
Magna Charta, 49, 50, 75
— — in Ireland, 131
'Manchester School,' 107
Manning, Cardinal, 29
Marshal MacMahon, 43
Mary I., Queen, 51, 139
'Masses' compared with 'Classes,' 60, 64
Maurice of Orange, 45
Michael Davitt, 18, 210, 215
Milton, quoted, 17
Mirabeau, 4, 17
Missolonghi, 271
Mobocracy, 78, 81
Montalembert, 68
Montesquieu, quoted, 44, 64, 65
Morley, John, on Home Rule, 201
Municipalities, 47
Murder of Archbishop of Dublin, 137
— of Lord Kilwarden, 167
— of Lord Frederick Cavendish, 191, 226
— of Mr. Bourke, 191, 226
— at Manchester, 190

NAPOLEON, 43, 111, 112
Nassaus, Dutch under the, 44, 45
National League, the, 218
Newman, Cardinal, 29
Nile Valley, x.
Normans, England under the, 49

O'BRIEN, 249
Ochlarchy, 41

Ochlocraty, **41**
O'Connell, Daniel, 168, 176, 198
O'Donovan Rossa, 187, 252
O'Kelly, 231
Oligarchy, 45, 127
— Irish, a curse, 140
Opportunism, Mr. Gladstone's, 154, 190, 195, 198
O'Shea, 26

PALMERSTON, Lord, 15, 102
'Papist Code,' the Irish, 152
Parliament, 47
— Irish, the, 156
— — in conflict with British, 157
Parnell, Charles Stewart, 22-25, 210, 215, 217, 225, 249
Parnell Commission, the, 241
Peace Preservation Act, 204
Peel, Sir Robert, 14, 70, 107
Peelite, Mr. Gladstone a, 11
Penal Laws, Irish, 152
People's Bill, 77, 90
Persia, **xi.**
Phaedrus, quoted, 245
Pitt, 101, 159, 205
Pius IX., 15
Plato, 57
Pluto-oligarchy, **41**
Poland, 101
Polignac, 43
Polybius, his ideal State, 39
— on Rome, **44**
Polygamy **in Ireland,** 128
Pope Pius **IX., 15; Hadrian IV.,** 129
Popery, 23, 29
Portal, Sir Gerald, **86**
Power, Mr. O'Connor, 210
Presbyterians, Irish, 155, 164
Press, the power of the, viii.
Prince John **in** Ireland, 131
Prisons Amendment Act, 113
Privy Council, 75, 94
'Protection Bill,' the, 214
Proudhon, 16

Prussia, the Herrenhaus of, 75
Puseyite, Mr. Gladstone a, 11

RADICALS, **xii.**
— their arms, **88,** 89
Rebellion of Emmett, 167
— of Smith O'Brien, 180
Redmond, Mr., 216, 230
Redmondites, 158, 234, 254
Regency Bill, 157
Reichsraethe **of** Bavaria and Austria, **75**
Reign of Terror, **43, 57**
Renan, 16
Revolution, French, 43, 57, 181, 265
Richard II. **in** Ireland, 133
Richard III. in Ireland, 134
Rights, Bill **of,** 53
— Declaration **of,** 53
Roebuck, Mr., **15**
Rome, decline **and** fall of, 271
Rome in the time of Brutus, 44
Rome Rule, Mr. Gladstone on, **246**
Rosebery, Lord, 235
Roses, Wars of the, 51
Russell, Lord John, 11, 15
Russell, Lord Odo, 100
Russia covets Constantinople, xi.
— has a friend in Mr. Gladstone, 98, 104
— always aggressive when Mr. Gladstone is in **power,** 99
— **aggression of,** 99-101, 105

SADLEIR and Keogh, 181
Salisbury, Lord, 87, 235, 241
Scandinavia, 255, 268
Shakespeare, quoted, 82, **126**
Schiller, quoted, 69
Scipio, 57
Sea, Black, **xi., 99**
— Red, xi.
Sebastopol, British army before, 15

Secret Societies in Ireland, 154, 167, 170, 171, 174
Sedan, 271
Senate of France, 40
— of United States, 40
Sinkat, 103
Sir Gerald Portal, 96
— Michael Hicks Beach, 16
— William Harcourt, 229, 234
Skirmishing Fund, the, 252
Solferino, 271
Sophocles, 17
States, United, 40, 155
Statute of Drogheda, 136
— the Kilkenny, 133
Strafford, Earl of, 4
Strongbow, 130
Suez Canal, the, x., 46
Switzerland, 40

Tacitus, quoted, 43, 46
Tanistry in Ireland, 128
Tarquin, 44
Tenure, Fixity of, Mr. Gladstone on, 222
Terror, Reign of, 43, 57
Tithes, Commutation of, in Ireland, 177
Tokar, 103
Tone, Wolfe, 228
Tonquin, x.
Town Moots, 47
Transvaal, 101
Trevelyan, Sir George, on Home Rule, 230

Tudors in Ireland, 136
Turkey, xi., 97, 100, 101, 104, 268

Uganda, 96, 101
Ulster, Colonisation of, 143
Uniformity, Act of, 141
Union, Act of, 160, 168
United States, 40, 98, 155

Vatican Council, 12
— Decrees in their Bearing on Civil Allegiance, 29, 153, 194
— and England, 23, 153
'Vaticanism,' 20, 153
Virgil, quoted, 82

Walpole, 84, 85
Walsh, Dr., 23, 246
'Walshite Inquisition,' 12, 158
Wars of the Roses, 51
Washington, 44, 46
Wentworth, 4
Westminster, Duke of, 241
Westport, Mr. Parnell at, 217
Wilberforce, 101
William of Orange, 51
William the Conqueror, 49
William the Silent, 45
Winchester, 48
Witan, 47
Witenagemote, 47, 48
Witt, John de, 45

Youghal, O'Connell at, 176

Zola, 16

www.ingramcontent.com/pod-product-compliance
Lightning Source LLC
Chambersburg PA
CBHW021958220426
43663CB00007B/865